The Angry Spectator

My thought, my irreverent thought, started on a golf course; a misplaced serenity where heaven and hell both occupy the same ground in constant near collision, singularly appearing and disappearing, depending on the flight of a dimpled ball.

It is a place where faith runs rampant, where one can actually believe the most unlikely physical accomplishments are about to happen. It has all of the measure of a place of worship, the game being a religion in itself.

A golf course is a cursed ground of curvaceous sensuality; skinned in green, white-sanded, and blue-watered. Dressed like a paradise, it lulls one into disbelief, as do all illusions and addictions. But it makes us believe in occasional miracles where all muscles and synapses come together in one gloriously orchestrated symphony of movement, where club head meets ball and the rising and descending line of the arc becomes poetry.

It has been a place where I empty my soul of all moderation, shame and civility. I came to the game only several years ago and quickly determined that God had no intention of my making it to His heaven or He would never have allowed me to hold that tool of the Devil—a golf club.

It is a gentleman's game, where I ashamedly have been no gentleman. Topping the ball incessantly, spraying it in all directions but straight, plowing into the ground behind the ball so hard it wrenches my shoulders, sending me yelling a scurrilous host of words and phrases that would make my mother cry in despair that she had raised someone so devoid of caring for the ears and sensibilities and upbringings of others.

In this landscape of heavenly beauty, on this June day, no miracles were being performed. The Devil again had the upper hand. I was starting to fume as my friend Jack Martin and I sat in our golf cart, silhouetted figures under a shading oak, while a foursome one hundred yards ahead was aerating the fairways, spraying sod like thatched missiles that landed so indecorously as only a piece of dirt-heavy sod can land; grass all askew, roots dangling, a wounded victim, lying like an insult on top of the meticulously mowed fairway.

On this ground where glory and despair walk hand in hand, and fantasy reigns, began a fantasy of thought about two men I have known all my life, but would discover I have never really known either one.

*

"I remember when I was immortal, don't you?" Jack mused. "But then I never knew what that meant." He was a man born to the argument even with himself. His voice loomed over and around our cart as it had for years in Atlanta's courtrooms.

I let his words roll around in my mind as I lazily stared down the fairway. I gave the statement no weight, responding as stupidly as I thought his remark was.

"You don't mean there is a possibility that you and I could actually leave this earth, do you?"

Jack shifted his athletic, six-foot frame in his seat, propped one leg up on the cart's dashboard and said with a serious look, "Oh, but the end is coming on like a herd of turtles, my friend. It's over. This party is just about over."

Jesus at 65

William Anderson

ALSO BY WILLIAM ANDERSON

The Wild Man From Sugar Creek

God's Arm

First Edition

ISBN: 0-6154-6515-3
ISBN-13: 9780615465159

Preface

The paths to discovering life's meaning and purpose are as many as there are humans. Some paths are short and clearly marked; others are a confusion of twists and turns. And to some this path is one without end where purpose is never found. This novel is intended for those seekers who are still on the path, still watching for convincing signs, who want, maybe even desperately want, to find the truth, but so far see it only in vague outlines. At some point a path must be chosen. *Jesus at 65* is about one's man's search for meaning and which one of many paths to take.

This novel owes much to one who made the choice and found the path to be clear and unequivocal.

*

William Anderson speaks and facilitates on the subject of searching for life's meaning as well as on science and religion. He can be reached at dub@andersonagency.net

His voice fit his rugged face, full like his sloping nose and pronounced cheekbones, and it was a firm voice catching your ear because of its preciseness.

I looked at him with some annoyance. "Are we on a shrink's couch? I could have sworn this was a golf cart. What's that crap all about?"

He shrugged. "You know I never had time for a midlife crisis. With time on my hands now, maybe I'm having a getting-old crisis."

I tried to cheer him up. "This is supposed to be play time, Jackster. You've made the big bucks. Got grandchildren. The house is paid for. You can travel, read books. This is the good time. You can smell the roses and swallow Viagra."

Jack had pulled a beer from a small cooler we stashed in a wire basket behind our seats. He pealed back the tab and it popped open, spraying fizz like miniscule white fireworks. He pressed the cold top against his lips, taking in a long first draw. "I handled turning forty pretty well, and fifty got my attention, but hitting sixty ended the fairy tale of always having the juice."

"The juice?" I responded.

"Yeah, you know, the drive, looking good, endless energy, the love of kicking butt and taking names."

Jack had been a partner at one of Atlanta's largest law firms. But this unyielding recession had caused his soft drink client to cut back dramatically on attorney hours. His billable time dropped so low after 2008 that the managing partner strongly urged him to leave. Law firms had become shark tanks where the sharks were eating one another.

He was sixty-five, had earned over $800,000 for years, making him fat in the wallet until the recession bombed his stock portfolio. He had recently built a two million dollar house at Lake Burton, just north of Atlanta. He had money left, but was now sailing before a weakened wind.

"So you're saying I'm going to lose my identity when I get too old to show up at the office?" I asked.

"Sounds like I've lost mine, doesn't it?" Jack mused. "I don't even know what to call myself. If I had a card, what or who would I say I was? How would I identify myself? I was called an attorney for forty years. Now what would you call me, a golfer? A retiree?" He said both with an obvious indignation, as though they were without meaning or degrading next to being an attorney.

"We could give you a new title. How about Links Lizard, or Honey-do List Manager?" I joked feebly. I had never had this kind of conversation with Jack. He had been seen on Atlanta television news shows for years; always brimming with conceit; ferocious in his assault on doctors whom he claimed had injured his clients.

He ignored my joking. "It's closing in on a year since I got the axe, and I'm probably better known on this golf course than the grounds keepers. I was a rainmaker at the firm. I was a lion when it came to generating business." He paused, and then with some bitterness said, "I used to lead the parade. Now I'm just a spectator."

"That's baloney. How many charity and company boards are you still on? You belong to three country clubs where everybody knows you." I protested. I wasn't in the mood for getting into a 'pity-me' discussion.

Jack ignored my entreaty to move off the subject. "Work was more important to me than I realized. My glory days are gone."

"But the good news for society is that there is one less lawyer to sue the pants off some poor doctor who then charges me more so he can pay for his insurance for protection from vultures like you."

Jack scoffed. "Wait until your surgeon cuts into the wrong disc on your back and all of a sudden your left side is paralyzed. You know the first phone call you'll make? It won't be to the doctor; it'll be to me to take every dime the doctor and the next ten generations of his family will ever make." He settled lower in the seat, satisfied with his rebuttal.

I could feel the phone pulsating in my pocket. It was my wife Callie. "You know I'm about to sink a 30 foot birdie. This better be good," I spoke in a golf announcer's hushed voice.

She sounded agitated. "You laugh about this, Sonny, but I don't think it's funny. David is lying spread-eagle on the roof again."

I turned to Jack, "You know this bonehead 21 year old son I've got? He likes to lie on top of our roof and stare at the sky. He says it empties his mind and allows the Voice of the Universe to speak to him."

Jack shook his head. "I think his head is already empty. He doesn't need to lie on a roof to prove that."

"I heard that!" she answered sternly. She repeated it even louder. Jack and I both smirked.

"Why do you get so upset? He's not going to fall off."

"You really don't understand, do you, Sonny? Yes, he absolutely could fall, but it's this whole Voice of the Universe nonsense. I think he has joined some cult." She sounded distressed and impatient with me.

"Cult? That is ridiculous. He's at that age where he's just trying to discover some truths. I think it's healthy."

"Healthy?" I no longer needed to hold the cell phone next to my ear. I had to calm this down.

"Ok, Honey, we're on the 18th hole. I've got to stop by the grill for a few minutes, then I'll be there and get him off." I shut up because I knew I was lying. I was going for lunch and that meant a beer and rehash of the game.

Callie normally had a smooth, even voice, but when she got upset, which was rare, her voice had a tough edge that seemed out of another body. Early on I found that yelling back at her set up a long and long-lasting anger. She could smolder way after the fire was out.

I thought for a moment after the call and said to Jack, "Our son has become his own man. He's driving his saintly mother crazy saying the Bible is for people who can't think for themselves. He calls himself a truth explorer. What truth he's exploring I don't know."

"He might explore getting a job," Jack mumbled.

David had graduated from Yale with a degree in business. It had cost me $150,000. And what does he want to do now? He wants to 'find the essence of the universe'. He can't start a career until he discovers the purpose of having a career or having anything. While he's searching, he thought he might want to start an organic farm. He said that was real.

I said to Jack, "He's like us. We're geared to run and what direction we're running in can be confusing to everybody, including ourselves. I know I get crazy if I have to sit still. Callie says it's because I'm lost; wandering without purpose in the wilderness."

I changed the subject. "Hey, did I tell you, I might have an offer to buy my company?" I had told none of my friends.

"I thought architects were all greeters at Walmart now," he said in a voice tinged with disbelief. "This damn economy has slammed anything connected with construction."

"I can't believe it either. But we redesign old buildings for graphic designers and IT start-ups. It's a good little niche we've been hiding in." I turned a tee in my fingers. "I guess I could work forever."

"One thing I know is that forever isn't as forever as it used to be." Jack said.

He got out of the cart and spread his arms in a stretch and turned his hips back and forth, building the muscle memory he would want when he teed off.

"I always hated the word *retirement*," Jack said. I have to admit, he didn't look like the kind of man you would ever find contemplating his navel. He carried an obvious energy with him. There was little bargaining with him. He knew the way. You didn't. But he had seemed slower lately. I had even noticed his breathing being a little labored. I always thought of his face as monumental with each feature its own prominence. All emphasized by his white-patched hair, combed back so that it looked full like a mane.

"Have you ever looked the word *retire* up in the dictionary?" he asked. "It says 'withdraw, go away, retreat'. And that ain't me. But for the past year that's what I've been doing."

I watched as the foursome in front of us came in and out of the woods, having found their balls which they then placed on favorable pieces of flat fairway, took their swings and watched the balls skitter along the ground or fly back into the woods. *Maybe we should ask them if we could play through*, I thought.

Jack took an easy swing with a hybrid wood. "Yeah, the rush of the courtroom was exhilarating. I will say there is a vacuum of sorts, a silence to the day when there are no more demanding clients, no more judges and juries to prepare a case for; you know, all the interaction and relationships that make up work." He waited a second. "Here's the problem: I used to know where I was heading for months in advance. Now I don't know where I'm going tomorrow."

I responded vacantly. "You need a map."

"No life coaches, please. No meaning of life discussions. What do I have 20 more years? I'd be eighty-five; that'd be a good age to check out. Hell, I could start another law firm, grow it, and sell it in that amount of time."

"Good news, Jack, the meaning of life for the sixty-something crowd is on your television every night. Just watch the commercials about the great 'silver years' and the 24-hour fun you can have if you take their vitamins or live in their retirement villages. It is life reduced to its most basic element; fun."

It was a sarcastic appraisal wrapped in my own growing belief that this life is a tragedy quickly played. My philosophy of life had become knowing love in all of its intensity and finding joy was about all we could ask for.

He took another practice swing that seemed to be more an expression of anger than trying to improve his game. "I despise the phrase *silver years*. I can't stand those good life commercials. It's a plastic world. Besides, I don't want to be around people that look like me all the time. That's why I quit going to our high school reunions; nothing but old people there. If I look that bad, I'm going to quit leaving the house."

I started noticing that after every swing Jack would puff his cheeks up and blow out in a long, quiet breath. He was getting winded over nothing.

"Hey, we're not running a marathon here. What's with the heavy breathing?"

He looked down the fairway and answered softly. "Yeah, I've been feeling weak for a month. Going in the morning to get checked out. Think I might need some iron medicine. We're all into body management now. Or number management. Blood pressure. PSA number. Cholesterol number. You should be given a calculator when you hit fifty for body counts."

"Don't worry. A man that's given the amount of money you have to our church is heaven-bound." Jack had been one of the deep

pockets every aggressive minister must have if they are about building a mega church, which our minister was.

"Heaven?" He responded wryly. "Won't it be a hoot if I've
given all of this time and money to get there, and the place doesn't
even exist?"

I tugged on my bottom lip. That was kind of an amazing
statement. He had been one of the go-to guys for fund raising, even
having a large, new fellowship hall named in his honor. "So what
the hell, no pun intended, have you been giving all that money for
if you think you've been buying a ticket to nowhere?"

"I'll have to be honest. Part of it is social. As you know, our
minister is a big mule in Atlanta. Our church has more CEO's than
a hundred corporations. Big steeple churches are like everything
else in life. If you want to play, you've got to pay. I enjoy the company of these people and am willing to pay for it."

I sensed that Jack trusted me far more than I'd ever thought,
or he would never have made such an admission. "So where is the
Father, Son, and that ghost in all of this?" I was truly curious if religion played any role in all of this posturing.

He shrugged. "I wish I knew where they were, Sonny. I keep
giving and thinking one of them will show up."

"Why don't we try Buddhism or one of those other religions?
Or try nothing. Just admit this is it. This moment is all we have.
Beyond that, who knows?" I felt a subtle anger in my voice. It was
a cover for the frustration and confusion and fear, downright fear,
I felt over being unable to find the answer on what my life was ul-
timately all about.

Jack and I were true skeptics. We had been rulers of our
respective worlds. We didn't look to a higher being; we were the
higher being. We controlled our domains like kings over their
kingdoms. But now he had no kingdom. He was a man in exile.

I looked idly down at the dash compartment of the cart and saw a new Titlist ball against something small and bright. Reaching in, I pulled out a bracelet with a cross attached.

"I don't believe this." I said in amusement. "Speaking of the Son, I think we've just had a message sent by the Big Golfer in the sky." I held up the small, silver cross that was looped onto a short, thin chain. It glinted in the morning sun as it dangled from my fingers. Someone had obviously taken it off and forgotten it after they had finished their round.

Watching it sparkle, I said, "Now here's an interesting thought...if Jesus lived today, would he have played golf? Talk about your miracle shots."

Jack asked, "You mean what would Jesus have done in retirement? Or better, what would Jesus have done on the back nine? Hey, I like that, Jesus on the back nine of life. Jesus at 65." He thought for a second, then asked, "Isn't that irreverent?"

One corner of my mouth turned into a slight, cynical smile; more a shrug. "Does it matter? Reverent. Irreverent. Who knows?"

Pointing his three wood down the fairway at the flailing foursome, he wondered, "Maybe we could ask the Lord to spray a little lightning around those sod busters and scare their butts off the course."

Repeating himself, Jack asked, "What would the Man be doing? Well, it wouldn't be golf," He thought for a moment and offered, "You know, I've heard about Jesus all my life, but I don't have a clue who he really was as a human being. Did they even retire back then? I didn't think they lived to be sixty-five."

"Jesus, the man nobody knows. But don't say that to my saintly wife. She'll put you on her prayer list."

Jack's brows furrowed. "Yeah, that's true. I've been worshiping—well, that statement wouldn't stand up in a courtroom—hearing about is more accurate, a guy I never knew as a guy." He reflected on what he had just said. "I mean he wasn't a real guy, was he?"

I found myself being as confused and as mildly amused about the subject as my friend. "I never thought about what he was like if you bumped into him on the street either. You know that Mona Lisa smile in all the pictures you see? Looked like an Englishman with blue eyes, long robe, long hair. Kind of floated along the ground."

"Like me, Sonny Boy, after a bourbon at the 19th hole," Jack grinned impishly.

The foursome finally walked off the 18th green 175 yards away. It was a water-wrapped, three-par nightmare, small in size and domed. You were either 'dead on' the flag, not just on the green, or the ball was rolling off toward water.

Jack bent over and pushed his tee into the grass. "Of course he didn't make it to old age, so it's kind of a pointless subject anyway."

I could see Jack's mind had melted back into the game. Erect and motionless, standing behind the ball, he faced the distant green as though his stance and stare would gain control of the ball's flight. His concentration could be wonderfully focused, and on this swing he hit a high-arching draw that dropped firmly at the green's edge. A straight line up the dome and into the hole awaited him.

"Now that's what I call heaven," he grinned as he pulled his tee up. "It's right here on this earth when you hit the right shot. And you know the sweet part is the sound. Hit the ball dead on and there is almost no sound. It's a click. You know I have a recording of that sound along with me putting and the kind of rounding, clanking sound as the ball goes in the hole. Got it on a CD."

"Ah, the meaning of life captured in a clank," I mused at his half-serious appraisal of how simple it is to find in life moments of sheer joy. Each is possessed of its own beauty. Hit a perfect golf shot. Throw a delicate fly-fishing line. Hit a cross-court smash.

Negotiate a high profit deal. Do a good deed. Maybe it's about accomplishing the difficult. Maybe it's about nothing. My mind had become squandered of thought, as thoughts have their own trail and their own way of disappearing, of being shouldered aside by another equally vapid thought.

"Start talking about the perfect man and you hit the perfect shot." I said.

Jack stood behind me while I addressed the ball with a hybrid club. I was thinking too much about my technique as I turned into the backswing. I didn't drop my shoulder enough when I drove down into the ball and slightly topped it, hitting a line drive that rolled into thick Bermuda twenty yards from the green. "Aw, the gods of the green don't like me today," I complained.

"Yeah, this is a battleground between the Devil and the Lord. Make a good shot and you say, 'Thank you, God'. Hit it in the rough, you start blaming the Lord, the Devil, and any other gods you can drag up," Jack mused.

"Enough of this religious talk; let's putt out and hit the grill."

"I'll drink to that," Jack agreed, as we headed for the 18th green.

The Grill

The clubhouse is a church where the worshippers of the fairways and greens come to hold service. But it is not a sacred place if sacred is where truth is an altar. The fudges of the ball, the slightest nudge away from a rock or root; where lies told are about the better lies slyly made.

If on a given day one's game has found redemption, communion is given with a cold beer and a BLT. If the devil ruled the course and the score card reads like a listing of sins, there would be much moaning and wailing, excuses and threats to quit the game, and more beers.

Either way the score card rules the room. It is the edict rendered by the Lord of the Fairways or the One God, whichever one serves. The card is a Rosetta stone translating the results of the swing, the trajectory of the shot, the vagaries of the winds, the nuances of the green. I held mine up as we entered the oak-paneled grill. I had shot an eighty, which was five shots under my handicap.

"Mulligan man," Max Baker shouted from across the room. His voice was slightly high pitched and out of sync, I always thought, for a man as tall and still muscular at sixty-eight as he was.

"Don't tell me the score. Tell me how many nudges to a better lie did you make when Jack wasn't looking. Look me in the eye and tell me a lie about your lies," Max laughed at his own poetry. He had a mouth like a large-mouth bass in its expansiveness, and it twisted and turned as he spoke, giving his words an actual physical look. Max didn't need his hands to make gestures; his mouth did it in a perpetual motion.

Phil Smith, whom we called 'The Reed' because he was not much thicker than the shaft on his clubs, sat next to Max.

"Jack, did Sonny cuss his way around the course again? How many clubs did he throw today?" Phil smirked, knowing how my temperament and this game were irrevocably incompatible.

Jack practically collapsed in his chair. The Reed noticed and mocked, "Hey, Jack, have you been giving blood on the course? Looks like you got your butt kicked."

Jack sat up straight and answered sarcastically, "We jogged the course and carried our bags."

We slapped our scorecards down like they were some certification of our athleticism. We both had scored well.

"Read it and weep, hackers," I smirked. "Honest to goodness, no mulligan, no fudging the ball. True scores."

"Well, praise the Lord, brother," The Reed raised his beer in a mock toast.

"Funny you would mention the Big Golfer," I said as I waved for the waiter to come over.

"Yeah," Jack joined in. "Funny what bizarre things you can discuss while you're watching the course being destroyed in front of you by true hackers."

"What things?" Max garbled through a whopping bite of his tuna melt sandwich.

I ordered a beer and a turkey burger. "We got to talking about retirement and I found this bracelet with a crucifix in the cart..."

"Oh, I see where this is going," Max broke in. "Two lousy golfers have a miraculous round of golf and suddenly they get religion."

"No, actually, and you'll love this, Max. I wondered what Jesus would have done if he had lived to be 65."

Max almost choked on the tuna, his face scrunched up as he exclaimed, "What!"

Jack had ordered a bourbon and Coke. A little heavy I thought, but he needed some mental emolument to crank down what looked like a growing depression over his life, or lack of it. He took a slow, appreciative sip and said, "Yeah, it was a very slow day on the course."

Phil said, "For you two to be talking about Jesus at anytime means it's a slow day."

"I'm the best Christian money can buy," Jack responded.

Jack's generosity was based in part because he liked Sandy, a very persuasive minister on a personal level. His being perceived as close to the powerful minister, along with his substantial donations, ingratiated Jack with the cadre of Atlanta's powerful whom the minister had cultivated.

Only he knew that he gave freely as a hedge in case there really was a God, and he wanted credit when credits were checklisted off in that intensely colorized place he envisioned as heaven; when he could even admit there was a real heaven.

My beer arrived in a frosted glass. The first taste of a very cold beer is like so much in life; the first time is the best time. I took a slow, thoughtful drink of its cold and its carbonation, before explaining, "Actually, we were trying to figure out what to do when we grow up. You know the 'R' word—*retirement*."

"What to do in retirement? That's easy." Phil had practically inhaled his BLT. He pushed the plate aside with its leftover crushed potato chip pieces. "Do Nuh-theeng." He smiled broadly as though the mere drawing out of the word was relaxing in itself.

"Nothing?" He could hear my disbelief. "So the reward we get for working our tails off all our lives, the payoff, is to be able to do nothing. We did something so we can do nothing." I took a second sip, while staring at Phil like he was nuts.

Phil nodded and smiled. "Hey! Don't knock nothing. Nothing is something, and it's good."

Fill the hours. I mulled over what sounded like an ordeal of emptiness. *Have our lives just been filling in hours?* I'd always been so busy building a company and a family I had never thought about not doing both. "So the end of work means that an empty life can be a full life? I'm sure there is a logic there somewhere."

Phil gave a sincere rebuttal. "Who am I hurting by hitting balls? Nobody. What about the word *enjoy*. What about just enjoy life and you get to define what that means."

Jack stepped in. "I kind of agree with Phil and kind of don't. Retiring gives us a choice we didn't have. And if that choice is to sit on your butt and watch grass grow or hit golf balls every day, then that's your choice. The real question is this: is watching grass growing the best way to spend the last part of your life?"

Phil answered with conviction. "You can knock playing golf, but I've found all the heaven I need and it's right out there on that golf course and here in this grill with my friends."

"That's until you make a bogey, then it's hell." I observed dryly.

Phil ignored my cynicism. "Heaven is hitting the sweet spot on a seven iron 160 yards out over water two feet from the hole." He smiled as though he could see and hear it all right now.

"Every shot is a test of mind and body. No game is the same. No shot the same shot. I'm around good buddies. Yeah, it's not solving the problems of the world, but at what point in my life am I supposed to stop feeling guilty if I'm not saving the world?"

Max ran his tongue inside his mouth, cleaning off the last of his tuna melt. "Said like a true godless man. You atheists do have a religion and it's either called fun, or in your case it's all science. But, don't worry, Phil, another world does await all of us. And you better get your butt in gear, or you'll spend eternity making triple bogeys on a course with one inch wide fairways."

Phil looked slightly dismayed. "Max, get your definitions right. I'm a nihilist and an existentialist."

"A what-ist?"

"Big guy, do you ever read about any ideas other than what's in the sports section? What about a little Kierkegaard or a few pages from Nietzsche?" Phil asked with exasperation, but a lot more condescension. "They are philosophers who said this world is without meaning or purpose. That's why we created morality and values to make it an orderly planet. It's up to us to find joy in this creation, in this existence, and not some spiritual myth."

Max scoffed, "Why do I want to read that crap?"

"I've read about those guys when I was in college," Jack said. "He's one of those that announced God is dead. Put me to sleep then; makes me sleepy talking about them now."

"Actually God never died, because God never lived," Phil said like he was making an announcement. "For fulfillment I drink at the cup of knowledge. Just learning is its own reward. Beyond that, believing that life has no inherent morality, no right or wrong, allows me to create the meaning of a thing. I create my own reality."

Phil had retired as a chemistry professor at Georgia Tech and was known nationally for his research articles.

Max looked at Phil, "Oh, so we can create our own meanings? Well your meaning is BS, skinny man. I don't care how many degrees you've got, you'll never figure out how this universe was created, and you'll never find true happiness until you accept the love of God."

"Whoa, boys. I thought we were here to discuss the fine art of bashing Obama like we usually do over lunch, not have a debate about religion." Jack had finished his bourbon and ordered another. I thought he was getting slightly slurry. Our lunches got into near shouting matches over politics, but never about religion before.

"Cool it, Jack. I'm trying to get this sinner to find wonder in God's creation," Max said.

"The only wonder I have is why ya'll believe this nonsense. No offense, boys. But it's not rational. And if there is any church I worship at, it's the church of the rational mind." Phil sat back, confident of his assertion.

Phil's skin stretched smooth over his prominent cheekbones. He had deep creases down either side of his nose to each side of his mouth. His nose was short and upturned and looked too pudgy to be on his thin face. His hair was close-cropped and neat in its growing grayness.

"Why don't we worry about all this when it gets a little closer to having to worry about it," Jack said.

"Well, that's about as shortsighted a statement as I've ever heard," Max groused. "Let's don't worry about whether God exists until it's time for us to cease existing."

Phil waved for another cold one. This was more than I had ever heard him talk about his beliefs or lack of any.

Max rested his chin on his left hand and looking at Phil said, "Skinny man, tell me this; do you ever doubt your doubt?"

Phil gave a breathy, short laugh. "That's good, Max. Does a doubter ever doubt his doubt? To be honest, I'll have to say yes. But only because I don't have the answer on what started the universe and what started life. Oh, and we still don't know exactly what gravity is or what consciousness is. If I doubt my doubts, it's always fleeting, because my belief in no belief comes quickly back."

"You know, Phil, since you scientists like to test theories, why don't you test your disbelief by doing a Christian act and see if acting like a Christian can bring you closer." Max offered.

"Oh, I know what you're doing. You're recruiting me to go with you on your next missionary trip to Malawi and install those wells. You're looking for a laborer."

Jack interjected. "If hard labor is a part of being a Christian, then stop praying for Phil's soul."

"Speaking of prayer," Max said with obvious seriousness, "I need for you pagans to pray for me and my business. I've got twelve houses finished and unsold. This recession is killing me."

Jack tried to downplay the gravity of what Max had revealed. "Just ask Obama for some of the stimulus money, Max. We'll all be working for the government soon."

Ignoring Jack's remark, Max confided, "I don't mind asking you guys to pray for me and my family. Yeah, you too, Phil. Make it up as you go. You know what the recession has done to construction in Atlanta. I haven't built a house in a year. Had to let my crew go. Half the conversations I have with Cindy are about cutting our costs. And you know one of the biggest expenses we have? The $1,500 I'm running up every month belonging to this club."

Max has been known as McMansion Max, having built some of the largest, most ostentatious houses in North Atlanta. He caught hell in the Atlanta newspapers for 'ruining the architectural integrity' of Atlanta neighborhoods. The size and grandiosity of his big boxes dwarfed the smaller, more charming homes next door. Many of the houses sat now in their unsold hulking emptiness. I knew he was being hammered on the loan paybacks on a number of these. Rumors of wholesale foreclosures on all of his spec houses were abundant.

I tried to sound sympathetic. "We're all being squeezed, Max, just in different ways." I had heard that his wife Cindy confided to her girl friends that they could no longer afford the club, and she was scared to death they were going to run out of money. Nevertheless, they were still having big cookouts and remained on the charity ball circuit.

Jack tried to add some levity to the conversation. "Well, we were speaking of Jesus, and you know he started a new career in middle age and didn't have a dime to his name."

"Yeah, but Jesus didn't like to play golf either," Max said and his broad, fleshy face finally broke into a grin.

"Yeah, and he could turn water into wine and feed 5,000. Who needs money when you can perform miracles," Phil added.

Max took a last bite from his tuna melt. His always-mobile face had a frozen stare. He suddenly spoke with a firmness uncharacteristic of his usual loquacious self. "I think we're all getting a little borderline with this retired Jesus talk, boys."

Jack thanked the waiter as our sandwiches arrived and said to me in a mock reprimand, "I told you Max wouldn't go for the old Jesus idea."

I waited on Max to respond. His voice had an unusual tone of finality. "The death of Christ is the most solemn and profound event in the history of man. I know we kid about a lot things, but saying Jesus wasn't crucified, that's over the line."

An uncomfortable quiet settled over our table. Then Jack explained, "Oh, no, he was still crucified. It was just thirty years later."

I explained, "Look, it was an innocent question about whom we could look to for retirement advice. Of course, he died in his thirties. But crucified at thirty-five or sixty-five, what's the difference?"

"There *is* a difference," Max firmly objected. "You're making a fiction out of the gospels in even talking about it, and this Christian doesn't like it."

Jack seemed a little miffed at Max's objection about even discussing the subject. "We're not saying he was never crucified. Lighten up, Max. You know the crazy stuff we talk about out on the course."

Max scoffed, "Well, the whole idea is crazy. I don't think retirement was a word back then, and did anybody even live to sixty-five?"

Phil said with a smirk, "As long as you didn't stub your toe."

For a reason I couldn't explain, I felt a renewed persistence about the subject. "Max, I don't know beans about Jesus, but you're the reborn one here. I would think you might be curious about Jesus if he hadn't died when he did, but died later."

"That's a clueless statement which really says how far from being a follower of Christ you really are."

Why did I feel it was such a corrosive statement? There was a hard reality about it that made me a little uncomfortable. Because he was right.

"So, no, I'm not real curious; don't want to be curious. These are sacred waters, and my boat on this subject does not want to be rocked." Max was resentful that I would be so casual about something of such profound importance.

I tried to move us back to what I care about and it was life after work. "Let's get back to our original subject, which is what are we going to do other than drink beer in this grill for the rest of our lives. As Jack asked earlier, what are we going to do on the back nine?"

"Beer in the grill for eternity. I could do that here or I could do it in heaven," Phil gazed upward as though contemplating an eternity of endless BLTs and cold Buds.

"What do you believe, Sonny? What's the purpose of all of this? You've been a deep pocket at your church. Does Christ have your back?" Max suddenly and pointedly asked.

I had been asked that question by my wife many times, by my mother, by any number of people in conversations at church, and it was like coming up to a door I couldn't open, or was afraid to open, because I really didn't know what was on the other side. Maybe I was afraid I would discover there was nothing there. I feared that was the answer, and I didn't want to know it. In the honesty of this moment I responded, "Do you mean what do I *want* to believe?"

Max leaned back in his chair and smiled knowingly, "Ah, the agony of the undecided. Is there a heaven, or is this it? A man who wants to think there is something out there, but whose rational mind won't let him sail across that void where faith becomes his wings."

My face always flushed when asked this question. It always made me confront a question I ran from, or to. "Everybody wants to think there's a point to all of this," I answered weakly. "And so do I."

Max persisted. He knew he had a waffler. "You're one of those guys who attends church and who is afraid to close his eyes during prayers, because he's afraid he'll fall asleep. Tell me, Sonny boy, do you believe that serving Christ is your purpose in life? Or are you the hypocrite I think you are?"

"Sounds like this Jesus boy has you in a headlock, Sonny," Phil grinned knowingly.

"So where are we in this rest-of-our-lives question?" I tried to take the focus off my answer and bring some order to the conversation. "We've got Phil whose got money, got time, and ain't accomplishing squat."

"Unless you want to call six handicapped golf 'squat'," The Reed quickly inserted.

"And we've got Jack The Downsized, a former big time attorney who is now managing his wife's grocery cart as he shuffles behind her at the Kroger store."

"And we've got me," Max pointed a thumb at his chest. "A home builder whose business has gone down the recession toilet. You might say I'm in forced retirement."

Phil couldn't resist. "Max, don't you believe in prayer? Just ask The Big Guy to send a buyer your way. The problem, my friends, is that this is a deterministic universe. The laws of physics leave little room for free will and a god whose mind you can change."

Max answered, "Wrong, atheist. It is a free will universe where we have options to do good or bad, but we can also ask God to lend a hand on occasion."

"Good or bad is what we determine to be good or bad. Neither exists. They aren't their own realities. Nature knows no code of ethics other than what we dream up. I guess that's why we call it nature. Whatever happens is natural, not right or wrong."

"Oh, yeah, remember to take me off the list about any older Jesus stuff you find," Max said. "You guys chase after that blasphemy. That's fiction, and the crucifixion and when it happened, is not fiction."

We had moved beyond the shallow waters of golf and into a conversation that had no bottom. Phil closed it down. "Okay, here's how we end up, boys. Sonny is going to figure out what Jesus would have been like at 65, and try and be like that. He'll fail miserably and consider being a follower of Muhammad. I'm going to be a man at peace with the gift of life and the knowledge to appreciate this most temporary wonder that nature gave me. Jack is going to remain confused about what he believes. He may die a fence sitter caught forever between heaven and hell. And Max, well, Max will lose all of his houses to the bank and lose, sorry, Max, even your golf membership and become a hitchhiking preacher to whoever will listen.

"All right," I instructed. "The next time at the grill it's back to Obama bashing and complaining about taxes."

As we stood to go our separate ways, Jack handed me a set of keys. "No making out on my bed." He raised his eyebrow in mock admonition.

"Oh, it'll be your bed specifically," I smiled. "I mainly want to see what's for sale around the lake and what the prices are."

He shook his head as though he were disappointed to tell me, "The prices are holding at Lake Burton. Not much under a million and that would be for an old cabin built in the fifties."

"I thought I'd take Callie up this afternoon, have a drink on your porch, watch the sun set over the water, and spend the night." I said.

"Sounds like a set up. Sounds like you haven't told her you want to drop a million on a lake house."

"Well, not a million," I grinned.

"I can tell you right now she's going to want to give any extra money to that mission in Haiti she's supporting. I would not want to be on my porch this evening, brother. There will be fireworks on the lake."

"Hopefully not," I answered with little enthusiasm.

Lake Burton

"Ah, my better-late-than-never husband." The beautiful Callie was standing next to the living room bay window when I got home after the game and lunch. She held a metal tape measure that rushes back into its container with so much urgency you think it's going to take your finger off.

"Does it take one hour to finish one hole? You said you were coming soon." She was annoyed and standing her full five foot nine, which she did when angry.

"Sorry, I got caught at the grill." And then trying to move off that sore point I quickly said, "I walked around the house; I didn't see your son on the roof."

"Oh, he came down a few minutes ago with this serene look on his face. He said he was one with nature." Her eyes furrowed. "Sonny, this is serious. You've got to talk to him."

"Callie, he's trying to find what this life is all about. It's nothing more serious than that." I was somewhat pleading, because I was ready to head for the lake. "I promise I'll talk to him and see what this is all about. But I think it's called youth."

"We need to run. I've got Jack's keys to their house and a bottle of your favorite Chardonnay chilled in the cooler. So let's go see how the deep pockets watch the sun set."

I had told Callie that we needed to start dating again; break out of what I felt was a gathering sameness about our marriage. But it was deeper than that. She had moved, become overcome, I thought, in her pursuit of religion. She didn't feel our marriage was in a rut, because, to me, she no longer thought as much about our marriage as she did her marriage to our church.

Seeing Catherine Reynolds for the first time was one of those near-death experiences that resets all clocks, remakes all plans, and reduces the tongue to a nonfunctioning muscle. Called Callie, she had walked into a jam-packed Friday night at a singles bar called Harrison's, and all sound stopped, all motion was stilled. She saw me at the same time and stood looking at me with an intensity that pulled me as though I were on a fishing line being drawn inexorably forward.

I had stopped in front of her. We stared at one another. Nothing was said. I put my hand lightly on her arm and guided her toward an opening at the bar. She and I were connecting at a primal level where words and moves are unwarranted intruders in the magical realm of currents from the heart.

"Chardonnay", she said softly. It would become a nickname I would call her for years afterwards.

She put the measurer down and got her purse, the small cooler with a fancy salad for supper, and a wrapped dish with cheese and jelly at its center for an appetizer. I picked up her overnight bag. "So I'm on time for the lake; what took you so long at the grill?" she asked.

As we headed for the door and the car, I half smiled and answered, "You won't believe it, but we wound up having a deep, no, a strange kind of conversation."

"Since when did you guys ever have a deep conversation in the grill," she kidded. "That grill exists of lives that orbit around a game of leisure. Anything beyond discussions about deep rough or deep sand traps doesn't exist." Then, seeing I wasn't sluffing off her remark, she asked, "Is somebody sick or did they lose their job, or...?"

"No, no, we started out talking about retirement and what to do, and I found this woman's bracelet with a cross on it in the cart. This got us to talking about," I paused, and I know sounding apologetic, I said, "Jesus."

Her laugh or snicker was laced with sarcasm. "You were talking about, who was that again? Surely you didn't say Jesus. Yes, I can see how that would be a strange topic since you basically only go to church for funerals and weddings. Oh, and let's not forget Christmas."

I answered weakly, "I find the Lord in other places."

"Of course. You find him hitting golf balls during the 10:00 church service. Yes, Jesus can really whack those balls on Sunday, can't he?" Her right eyebrow was cocked, and she gave me that knowing stare.

I didn't respond. She was on the attack, and I was trying to keep things low key before we got to the lake.

"So I guess the strangeness was that you, and especially that heathen friend Jack, were talking about Jesus at all."

"Okay, Okay. It was odd only because we were wondering what Jesus would have been doing if he hadn't been crucified so young but had lived to, say sixty-five and then died."

Callie's lips pursed together, and she blew air between them in a silent whistle. She then asked, "So when you finally talk about Jesus, it's about what if he had lived to be an old man? Well, I guess it's better than nothing."

Pausing, she concluded, "I think we are experiencing a delayed mid-life crisis."

"Well, I've been in delayed childhood all my life, so I guess it's time to grow up. Amazing what nearing sixty can do to you," I acknowledged in the jesting way we goaded one another.

Poking me on the shoulder, she said, "Excuse me, is this one of those meaning of life moments? The big 'Six O' has rattled my feelings of immortality? Like, whoa, I can see the end of this tunnel called life and I'm not sure if that light at the end isn't a truck."

"Give the man no credit for discussing your favorite subject," I countered. "So now that I'm no longer a child, does that mean you'll stop treating me like one?"

"Probably not," she smiled, answering truthfully. "After all, you are a baby boomer. Doesn't that mean you're stuck in a kind of perpetual, pathetic childhood?"

"Well, I could get a walker and start drooling if that would make me look more like my age."

Callie responded, theatrically raising her arms up and shouting, "Hallelujah, my husband is interested in finding out about Jesus being an old man, although every human on the planet knows he died young. Will you keep your findings in the family, please? That's the kind of a squirrelly subject matter that our friends might give a big 'What?' to."

Callie loved to kid me, and she was kidding now to suppress her surprise and because she didn't know quite what else to say.

Lake Burton has been a fixation with me for years. It, and its sisters, Lakes Rabun and Seed, are the jewel of the Georgia mountains for a second home. Its waters lie deep between oak and pine covered hills; no longer mountains really, but the ancient remnants of a sky-piercing range that once looked like the Rockies.

The area has that feel of permanence and oldness that can be translated into grandness and elegance. Bold, Burton isn't. Relaxed and understated it is. I had always wanted a place there, no obsessed about it, to be a part of that silken lake world; those afternoon cocktail gatherings in boats, the chit-chat, the white loose cotton dress; all this ethereal setting on glass-smooth, tree-green water.

We turned off the highway after an hour and a half of driving up from Buckhead. It was 5:00. A narrow road leads to the lake area. The June sun was merciful and not overbearing as it had been the day before. Burton and its sister lakes Rabun and Seed were built in 1919, filling the gorges cut by the Tallulah River. The river was damned so power could be generated.

It was a rustic area. Home sites had to be leased from Georgia Power. It was early in the century, before vacation homes became overstatements. So the first places built were simple cabins. Today wealth rings the lakes with competitive, ostentatious homes situated above boat docks that preen like small cottages.

I was carefully checking for phone numbers on the occasional 'For Sale' sign we would pass. But I had already heard about a home nearing foreclosure, and if Callie liked my idea of owning a home here, we would find it. We pulled up in front of a quaint wooden sign that read 'Tort Land'. It was the short, dirt driveway to Jack's house. Callie and I had been there before, but never as though it were ours alone and never witnessed in its early summer dress of perennial flowers declaring their colors.

Jack's lake home was a three story, 5,000 square foot attempt at cottage quaintness, if that much square footage can be called quaint. Its enormity for the small lot did have that straw hat with a bow kind of look. Pale blues. Bright yellows. White planking sides. Trellises were covered in confederate jasmine vines, arched so that you had to walk under them to the back door, as though you were making a grand entrance. And inside the great room were wicker chairs of soft earth tones with the entire area accented by pops of yellow and darker blues against white board walls.

We put the food on the granite kitchen tops, and our overnight bags next to a floral covered sofa.

I watched as Callie strolled through the room, ran her finger over the fabric on the chairs and smiled as she drank in the perfect placement of sofa, table, vase, paintings and accessories.

"Pretty terrific, huh?" I meant it, but I was also trying to quietly get her mind in the mood for what I was going to tell her later.

She answered without looking at me. "It couldn't be more beautiful." She almost purred. Then her voice came back with a discernible edge, "If this is how you want to spend your money."

I acted like I didn't hear the last remark. "This life has good times written all over it. What's more important than spending your money on family and friends?"

Before she could counter my soothing words, I said. "Hey, let's break out that dip you made and I'll open the wine. That porch looks awfully inviting." I moved toward the kitchen area at one end of the large living room as Callie wandered out onto the teak wood flooring of the expansive porch.

The center of the lake was diamonded with an angling sun.

The hills bordering the water are more like ocean swells in their gentle roundness. They are laden with thick firs and hardwoods, giving them a deep green coloring that throws its hue out onto the lake in dark reflections.

We sat and talked, swiped into her avocado dip with thick, salty chips, and soon felt the glow off a fruity cabernet I had brought. As the afternoon sun was setting cloud streamers afire to the West, it was time to make my proposal. I had to play it from how it would benefit her, not me.

Summoning up an energetic, enthusiastic voice, I turned in my chair to Callie's, touched her wrist and said. "You know I've got a good chance of selling the company, and we should clear about a million and a half from it. If you put that on top of the IRA we already have, we'll be in good shape. It means we'll have money to put toward your Haiti mission and a lake house that gives you a great place for church retreats."

The air was tinting the sun's light, casting her face in a subtle orange that reminded me of a time when we were hiking outside Santa Fe. Afternoon light can have a makeup quality, like rouge that fills in creases and wrinkles and for a fleeting time restores a youthful allure. A light bath. The sun's apology for its years of damage.

Callie lowered her sunglasses and cut her brown eyes toward me in a classic look of skepticism.

"Well, that's pretty big news. Getting away from sixty hour work weeks will give you all sorts of opportunities." She paused. "But what is this retreat business about?"

"Callie, a dream I've always had is to own one of these lake homes at Burton. I've found a house that may be close to foreclosure. I think I can get it for about $600,000. It's a million dollar house and online it looks like two million. We can look at it when we leave."

My brilliant revelation, all to her benefit, was not met with a schoolgirl's enthusiasm. Now the Callie moment of silence where her mind is filling with 'Is he crazy?' thoughts. But she was gaining control; I was a witness many times to this internal role-playing, word-testing; a mind at warp speed thinking of the best, most effective, most convincing way to express itself without sounding angry or forceful.

"Sonny McGrath." Anytime she started a sentence with my entire name I knew the rest of the sentence was not going to be beneficial to me. "I am one of the leaders in building a school for orphans in Haiti. You know that. I have spent time and energy there. We are in a fund drive to finish it. This amount, this $700,000 would finish the school and over one hundred desperate children living in the streets would have a home."

She continued calmly. "I appreciate (no she didn't) your saying, and you're right, that we could have great retreats here for the church. Not to mention the fun you could have, or our family could, with a home here. I'm sure it's beautiful, Sonny. But think of the lives the orphanage could change forever."

I knew I was sailing now against a headwind. My dream lake house was being buffeted. The mystical deep green waters, the great homes, the unique boat houses and the residents in their summer whites, their cool, their knowing, their connections and boards, all accomplished people and all interesting, all fun and funny. I had always been just outside that crowd, the really *in crowd*. It was a glow they lived in, and I wanted to live in the glow. Okay, call it all ego. I didn't give a damn. It was where I wanted us to be.

I felt flushed but careful in my response, since this conversation could flame out just like the teetering sun.

"I know how important the orphanage is to you and to those children. But Haiti is like a bottomless pit, Callie. Money just disappears there. What happened to those millions after the earthquake? It's a hopeless place. Why can't you focus on America's needs? Have charity meetings here at the lake? Why not help Appalachian people?"

"Jesus said, go out unto all the nations." She answered.

I interrupted her flow. "Well, I could say Jesus said to go to Lake Burton. Don't the rich have to be ministered to? One wealthy redeemed soul can make more impact on this world than giving the same money to a hundred homeless people."

I was in her face with my temper. But I meant it. I was burned out with Callie and our church's endless admonitions about flying all over the world to spend a week with people we would never see again in our lives. I saw my wife as blinded by this 'all nations' commandment. These long distance mission trips seemed a little self-serving and overly pious, even patronizing to me. I had become cynical about the trips and I knew it. I had found myself digging in on being challenged about purpose and mission in life. I found myself clinging to the way we were. Callie said I was immature and was living in the past. Her anthem had become 'Let go and let God'.

She ran her tongue inside her upper lip. It was her way of counting to ten. She had a point to make and however hot I got wasn't going to stop her thought. "The need is so great in Haiti. I've now been there five times. My heart breaks for those children, Sonny; they're starving, abandoned. There is no big United States-like government and rich people to help them." And then she played her main card. "I feel God has called me to build this orphanage. And with your help I can fulfill God's will for me."

Callie smiled that broad, beatific, thin-lipped smile that meant she was at peace with whatever she had just said. Her hand touched mine. Where was I to go after that? After the smile. The hand touch. After the statement that God wanted me to forget my dream house at Burton and to give my money to Earth's greatest failure, Haiti.

While I mustered my response, she interjected, again in that voice designed to convince through its gentility.

"We're getting to the age where what we do with our time takes on an urgency. We have to have a renewed purpose, a mission that is beyond our own selfish needs. Sonny, we have a freedom to do good that we never had before."

She was painting me into a corner. To have a dream home was to do badly. To give the money to a sink hole was to do good, or at least I saw Haiti as incurably corrupt with a population hopelessly despondent. The challenge of an admittedly narcissistic man

who marries a selfless woman is to be forever, however subtly, reminded that he is a self-serving, unconscionable cad.

She looked at me with concern and earnestness. "Sonny, now
is the time to find a renewed purpose and meaning to your life.
Selling your company can impact hundreds of lives." She shivered
like she was chilled. "I get tingles all over thinking about how this
can give a renewed meaning to your life."

This is pretty pathetic, I thought. Our marriage comes down
to Jesus and what he has told my wife to do with our money. Callie
would say it comes down to what is meaningful, to the big questions like what imprint does our life leave? The heavy stuff that I
had always avoided. I preferred to play in the moment. And I wasn't
going to cave.

"You're right, of course," I admitted. "How do I justify sitting
on my deck drinking wine and mixing it up with friends when I
could give refuge to a hundred kids? But why is purpose only good
if it's always measured by great acts of humanity? Why can't meaning be found in friendships and just having laughs?"

She got up and walked to edge of the porch, a vision in the
glow of the light from the sun settling into embers as the day relin-
quished its hold behind her. She was still tall, still trim, her neck
elegant and long. Her face was small, but with wide-set eyes, dark
brows and a wide mouth. Now 60, Callie remained a looker.

"Let's do something noble." It came as an announcement, a
clarion call said with emphasis and urgency. "Let's take the days we
have left and make an impact. That is what God has asked of me,
and I only wish you would be touched as I have. I only wish you
could find Christ and the joy he offers."

"Callie, I am not Mother Teresa. You know that I have big
problems with faith, any religion. I'm skeptical by nature. I place
great value, and I don't mind saying it, on having an independent

mind. I'll give to the orphanage. I'll even go down there and help build it. But this world, the world that revolves around this lake, is filled with much of the essence of life that make me a happy person, and that is good times, great conversations, laughter, and supporting those you love. I make no apologies for it."

We both sensed this conversation could quickly deteriorate.

"Listen, we've both made our points. Let's just cool it on this subject and enjoy the rest of the night. I've got a movie…"

"Forget it. Let's go home," she interrupted curtly.

"We just got here." I protested.

She walked away from the deck's edging, brushed by me as she headed for the sliding doors opening into the house. "Still trying the old get-the-girl-drunk trick, huh, Sonny?"

I turned as she went by. "The old what?"

"Give 'em a little wine, a pretty sunset, and they'll say 'yes' every time. We didn't come here to enjoy a sunset. We came for you to sell me on your buying a lake house." With that, said calmly and knowingly, she disappeared into the great room and picked up her overnight bag.

That comment really steamed me, probably because I had been caught in a lie which no one likes to admit. I walked quickly into the great room and followed her across the floor toward the back door and our car. "Oh, I see it now on the divorce papers; reason given for the divorce: 'Jesus'. Jesus wanted Haiti, the Devil wanted the lake house."

She kept walking out the back as she said, "And that's about the fraternity boy response I've come to expect from you."

I grabbed the food, still in the small cooler, and followed like a small dog that had just been reprimanded by its owner.

Silence can have its own sound, and our car pulsated with it as we drove the hour and a half back home.

That night I lay in bed listening to Callie breathing in the deepness of her sleep and wondering why, when I closed my eyes, that darkness did not sift over me and carry me away on its quiet wind. But tonight there was no room for an intruder like sleep. My mind was filled with the divide that had come between us, a divide filled with the promise of widening even more.

Mr. Charlie

The lake trip had been bruising. We said those mechanical things necessary to run a house for most of the rest of the week. One thing I had forgotten was the whole discussion about Jesus as an older man, or my retirement. We were on a deadline for drawings to go to a county commission in South Georgia; another old courthouse ready for restoration with the federal stimulus money. My mind had been safely sequestered at work.

But on Saturday morning before I left for The Creek Club and a round of golf, Callie surprised me with breakfast in bed. She said she was sorry about all that happened at the lake. She wanted to let it lie, see if I could even sell the company, then we could revisit what to do with the money.

I loved her mightily at times like this, and felt I should have made that first move. But that was Callie, and this was me, usually trailing behind in her wake of forgiveness and rectitude.

After a long hug, we rarely had long kisses anymore, I headed for The Creek. I was in the pro shop signing up to play when one of the assistant pros saw me and came over.

"Mr. McGrath, didn't you turn in a bracelet with a cross on it last weekend?"

I stopped, a little puzzled about why he would ask that. Then answered, "Well, yes, I did."

"I don't know if you know Mr. Charlie, but it was his and he wanted to meet the man who returned it."

Why the big thanks? It was a simple silver cross, if it was even silver, on a bracelet chain. Not an expensive piece of jewelry at all. "Don't believe I know Mr. Charlie. Is he a club member?"

"Well, sort of. His family sold the land and their home for what became The Creek Club. But he hasn't been here in years. I didn't even know him when he came in."

"Really? Must be a hundred."

"I heard he was 87 and thinks a golf club is a tool of the devil. Somebody said he might be a preacher. He's out on the deck at the pool. I think he's waiting for you."

"Waiting for me?" I was a little incredulous. I had never heard of him, and how did he know I would be coming in this morning?

I started not to look for him. My mind was on the day's round, and I wasn't in the mood for a sermon. I assumed he was a retired minister testing the flock with the hokey idea of leaving crosses around. But as I bought a package of tees, I looked out the windows that allowed a partial view of the pool area. Sitting under an umbrella I could see a broad shouldered man sitting very erect with his back to me.

He turned in his chair, looked toward me with a shadowed face, nodded his head, and turned back. He was wearing a wide brimmed sun hat.

What was that about? I almost wondered aloud. *Does he know me?*

I felt compelled, drawn, pulled; something, to walk out and meet him.

It was the kind of fresh June morning when there is such a clarity it's like there is no air; no nothing between your eyes and whatever you look at. Everything is accentuated in an ultra-reality of detail. The kind of day you can count the leaves on trees from a distance.

The cleats on my golf shoes clicking on the pool decking reminded me of high school football when we players, feeling like self-proclaimed heroes, clattered out of the locker room and out onto the field. There was an enormous nostalgia I always have had for that sound. There is something authenticating about it, known only by those who have worn the cleats as young warriors.

"Mr. Charlie?" I inquired in a ridiculously obsequious manner as I approached the shadowed figure under the table's umbrella.

He turned his head toward me, not getting up. "I am." His voice was certain without the quivering and high-pitched sound of many his age.

For some reason I stayed, standing out in the glare and looked into the shadowed table. I could see his face was full with a prominent nose, but his brows were so dark and overhanging that I couldn't see his eyes clearly. The rim of his hat cast a further darkness over his face.

He didn't invite me to sit, and child-like, I remained standing a few feet from him. We didn't shake hands, as both of his hands remained placed on something in his lap.

"I understand you wanted to see the person that found the bracelet. Well, that's me." I think I sounded a little overly eager.

"You aren't prepared to carry what you returned, are you?" His voice was capturing, firm, but consoling.

What? Is this guy some kind of mystic? His question was so out of left field that the only thing I could think to say was, "I would hope someone would return something I had lost."

"What have *you* lost, Sonny?" he asked. His head remained turned toward me though the rim of his hat and the glare of the day made his face still somewhat vague.

"Lost? Nothing I know of." *Did he say my name?*

"I think you do."

Who is this guy? I felt a growing annoyance at the audacity of the man, whoever the hell Mr. Charlie was, or thought he was.

"Look, I've got a club tournament I'm playing in. Glad to return the bracelet. Have a good day." And I started to turn and leave.

He ignored my remark and said, "Most days are not clear. Most days the air is like a liquid you're looking through. I like a day when there appears to be no air between my eyes and what I'm looking at. I like clarity."

He said what I had thought when I walked out on the deck. So now he's a mind reader? I turned back toward him. "So what is this I've lost that you're talking about?"

"Actually, you've never really found it. Some don't have to try at all. But others have to throw out a big net. You might consider that." He said with no other explanation.

Callie has accused me many times of having an absurd temper. And I could feel it rising. It always starts at the back of my neck like warm water turned on and flowing upward and over the top of my head until my face flushes with its heat, which is what it was doing now.

"Tell me this, Mr. Charlie. Just who are you, the club wise man?"

He didn't say anything for a moment, either controlling his own temper or collecting his thoughts, who knows. Then patiently, "I'm sorry, I'm holding you up. Your game is more important. Thank you for returning the bracelet." And he turned away and his fingers rummaged over what I could now see was the bracelet. His thumb ran up and down the tiny cross.

I shook my head. *Was he trying to put a guilt trip on me?*

To hell with it, I thought, and turned and started walking away.

His voice came back to me like it was from a longer distance, that soft sound you hear on a lake when fishermen are talking out in the water. "Remember, throw out a big net."

Throw out a net; is that what he said? What net, and to catch what? I walked away, shaking my head in exasperation. My curiosity made me look back at the table as I got to the door that led into the club, but he was gone.

We had a great round that morning. My 85 was, for my erratic game, a thrill. How can a game be so uplifting and at the next swing be equally damnable? Why do I pay so much money to be generally unhappy?

It may be one of life's endless absurdities that the click of the club's face against the ball elicits feelings of utter joy, completeness and surrender that must be akin to a spiritual experience. If there's something mystical, or metaphysical in becoming one with a perfectly hit ball, then I have, on rare occasions, found this subtlety called spirituality.

The Odyssey Begins

Faith is a winding stream. It flows strong and straight in places, then swerves and eddies and meanders indecisively. With faith we can have both belief and disbelief almost washing over one another, being as faithful as we are faithless.

Into this constant intrusion of our doubt and equivocating, Christianity counters by being an ambivalent taskmaster, at least to me. It allows for slippage into a multiplicity of sins by offering grace. Yet it mandates no slippage, no endless sinning, but purity through a singularity of thought, total conviction and intentionality. One God. Love. Service. Forgiveness. All maintained through faith, but faith so strong that it becomes reality.

I have been unable to yield my freedom of thought to what appears a form of servitude to a Taskmaster. Place the blame at the feet of rationality. I am in a business of proof, of facts, of unerringly accurate measurements. The buildings I design rely on the details of knowing materials and weight loads. I cannot tell a client they should move into my building with the faith that it won't fall. Certitude is my mandate.

My wife has long fled the land of doubt. The loving God of the Bible and the exquisite caring of Jesus are her comforts and her springs of strength.

Callie is one of those planks that a church that's growing must have. Her involvements, her innovative programs, are so recognized that she is not just called friend, but example.

The Bible and its scriptures are the sun that rises on her every morning. She reads it quietly while I roll over for another dream. We have become faith versus facts, and it has taken some of the oil out of the engine that drives our marriage. Should I say God has come between us? I can see it in the news, *Man Gives Reason For Divorce: Too Much Jesus.* Callie wouldn't think that was funny.

It was my night to cook, and I was making turkey burgers for the grill. You can't lay ground turkey directly on a grill or it sticks to the heat and comes apart when turned. So I mix the meat with mayonnaise and olives and chopped onion and set the patties on aluminum foil.

"What a partner!" Callie exclaimed as she walked into the kitchen. "Low fat and good, and I don't have to cook."

"Or wash the dishes," I proclaimed.

She kissed me on the cheek. "You are the bestest."

I summoned up a little courage while squishing ground turkey between my fingers. "I wanted to run something by you again that I brought up a while back. As you know, I'm a work in progress on religion."

She patted me on the head. "Not much work and very little progress."

"Very funny, and not very encouraging. Your turkey burger just might get burned." It was the nature of our relationship; harmless banter forever kidding, but too much of our kidding was filled with truth.

"Remember when I told you about looking up some information on Jesus as an old man? For some reason I'm still interested. I mean, if you had asked me a week ago I would have said I really don't care what Jesus could have been like at 65. So I guess I'm more puzzled about why I'm interested in something I've never been interested in. Okay, don't say it; I'm the first to admit that I'm no student of the Bible."

"A vast understatement," Callie interjected with confidence. She paused then asked with a sincere curiosity, "Sonny honey (her nickname for me), we've gone to church for our whole marriage, but we both know deep down that you go half because of me and half because you get to visit friends. So why when you finally show an interest in Jesus, it's this absurdity about his being an old man? Perverted isn't the right word, but sacrilegious sure is."

"It started when Jack and I started talking about retiring. My interest in the subject was not how Jesus would have retired, but how I'm going to retire; what am I going to do with my time? I think it's starting to kind of freak me out. I look into the future and see a big void."

Callie looked confused. "We have had a lot of conversations about selling the company. You thought it would be a freeing experience. You could read all the books you never did, maybe even take college classes, paint, play golf. You jumped at the chance. We wrote out a long list of all the things you could do when the company was sold."

"I know." I smiled wanly, "Sounds like I'm running from one fear to another."

"Ah, the angst of the elderly man."

"Cute. Not elderly yet, I hope."

"A rose by any other name is still…"

"Hey! Chill with the old man talk." I interrupted. "It's a cinch you'll never make it as a psychiatrist."

"Only kid-ding," she rolled the word out so it sounded like she was pleading. "Something has moved you about this more than your being worried about retiring."

"Actually, it has gotten a little weird. It started with my finding that bracelet with a silver cross on it in our golf cart. That's what started the conversation between Jack and me, just casually, about Jesus. We then went into the grill and talked more about it with Max and Phil. Then I forgot about it until I ran into a man at the club that the bracelet belonged to."

"What man?"

"Everybody calls him Mr. Charlie. His family actually sold the land and house to The Creek 50 years ago."

"And…?"

I didn't want to anoint Charlie with some mysterious air so I sluffed off our meeting. "He told the pro shop that he wanted to meet whoever had turned the bracelet in. I met him at the pool. He acted so strange that I got fed up and left. He thanked me for returning the cross, but he seemed like some wack job."

She looked confused. "I don't know what to make of that, but I wish you would drop this whole idea. Honestly, it would be embarrassing to me if some of my Bible study group found out about it."

I could feel an immediate anger rush up the back of my neck. *Embarrassed? That's what turns me off about religion; there's not much room for exploring. Shut your mind down. Just read the Good Book and go to sleep intellectually.*

"This isn't so much about Jesus as it is my thinking about ideas for retiring and the Jesus idea just kind of tagged along to that." My anger was masked.

"So, are you going to read some books about it? How will you go about this?"

"I've gone on Amazon and dropped by the library, but books about Jesus as a man, not to mention in retirement, are as scarce as the number of hole in ones I've made." I had finished the patties, wrapped them in a blanket of tin foil and started for the back porch. Callie followed.

"Then how will you get your information?" she asked.

"I'm clueless. I don't know except to start calling our minister Sandy and the universities around Atlanta and just asking for professors who might specialize in the history of that period. I'm pretty much stumbling along on this one."

"Well, I wish you would stumble in another direction." Her dark brows turning downward reflected her dismay at my venture.

Over the next several days I was turned down by the first of two theologians I reached. When I asked if they would be willing to discuss Jesus living longer, one's response was, "Well, that's a pretty stupid idea. I want nothing to do with fictionalizing the most important moment in history." No goodbye, just click. The second was, "Who knows and who cares." Click again.

Life impedes. Intentions trip over its erratic nature.

With the early rejections to my attempts at interviews, I almost let the idea slide once more. But whatever was pushing me on this pushed again. I found a professor at Emory University's Candler School of Theology who mumbled, "Yeah, come on in and bring an example of your writing."

Fence Sitter

The bronze plate read, 'Dr. Mathias (Matt) Gordon'. His door opened to an office that looked as though a hand grenade fight had just taken place with papers frozen in half flight off his desk and stacked with abandon against the wall.

"Dr. Gordon?" I asked quietly, reluctant to interfere with his concentration on a paper on which he was writing.

His dress was in contradiction to the chaos of knowledge spilling out of a small library of books and a discordant forest of paper. He was fastidious in a starched, pinpoint white shirt and a green and blue striped tie. His graying hair was thinned, but neatly parted and combed. His face was pleasant, but uneventful. He waved a hand for me to sit, and said with obvious impatience, "What was this about again?"

I leaned over his desk, shook his hand, and sat in a wooden chair in need of a softening cushion. "Thank you for seeing me," I offered as a form of, 'hello'. "It was about an older Jesus."

"I only remember vaguely. What do you mean an older Jesus? You mean he wasn't crucified?" Then he intently stared at me and declared with some surprise, "You don't look like a student."

"Lord, no. That was forty years ago. And my interest is not Jesus not being crucified at 35, but years later at 65." I politely corrected, smiling as I did.

"Crucified at 65? Why that's speculative nonsense." He was looking down at a copy of his note from my call. "Oh, yes, I see that here."

His gray eyes were set on me with great suspicion. "Few in any theology department would discuss the speculation of a delayed crucifixion. Now I do remember that you're curious if an older Jesus could be a guide for today's retirees. That may be interesting to you, but it's a line of thinking I abhor." His face had lost some of its pleasantness. His eyebrows arched downward.

My heart made a slight skip. Did he agree to see me so I could get a roasting? "I'm certainly not trying to be sacrilegious," I responded.

"Are you a convicted Christian?" He asked in what was more an accusation than a question.

Pausing, uncertain of how open I could be, I answered truthfully, "No, I'm not convicted. I'm not even convinced I am a Christian at all."

"Have you been baptized?"

"Actually, when I was eight years old, the minister said all who would like to be born again come on down. I had no clue what he was talking about, but went down and had water sprinkled on my head."

"That was absurd. Going through the motions. I get so sick of churches and religion," he scowled. His eyes narrowed at me. "I must admit I didn't think through your request to see me, or I wouldn't have agreed for you to come in. I guess I thought you were a divinity student. I don't mean to sound rude, or close-minded, but I have no time for fictionalizing the sanctity of the crucifixion. It is much too precious to play with."

I was afraid my visit was about to quickly end. "I appreciate that," I said with some energy. "I do know Jesus commanded his disciples to go out and tell his story to the world and not just speak to those who already believed. What you tell me could conceivably make a positive impact on my friends."

"So they are nonbelievers, or play-like Christians like you seem to be."

"One is an atheist, the other an agnostic who wants to believe, and the third is a true believer."

"And you sit safely on the fence," he correctly surmised.

"Tell you what, I need some fortifying to get through this. Let's have a little fellowship." With that he leaned down and loudly opened a cooler as I could hear ice being scooped up and dropped into glasses. He rose with two glasses, then opened a desk drawer and pulled out a bottle of gin and small bottle of tonic.

I almost never drink during the day, and had no desire to drink gin with a man I didn't even know. "Oh, thanks, but I've got work to do today, so I'd better pass it up."

His eyebrows dropped in anger for a moment; then he seemed cheered and sat about pouring the drinks. "Oh, a little drink before lunch is good for you." Pausing, he continued, "It's difficult for me to stop the utter belief I have in Calvary and imagine that Pilate had never ordered the crucifixion. And discussing that sensitive subject with a man I don't know makes it even more difficult." He then asked, "By the way, what do you do for a living?"

He was playing me. I knew a heavy drinker when I saw one, and this conversation was going nowhere unless I took that drink. I should have gotten up, but I caved. I reached for the drink, and with him watching carefully, I took a sip.

Turning his wrist, he looked down at his watch, breathed out in resignation and said impatiently, "Okay, I've got twenty minutes, gentile, or is it pagan? You'll be my discipleship work for the day. Maybe if you can get to know the man you will want to know the Christ." He then quickly finished his drink.

"I draw up the plans for restoring old buildings. I'm an architect. I appreciate good design and the cross is one of the best ever.

Simple. Elegant even. Clean lines. Certainly the best known brand on earth."

The professor mused rhetorically, "Well, that's a step in the right direction. At least you like the symbol of our faith. I'll tell you, I truly love that cross for all of its horrors. Where would our faith be without the cross?"

He then frowned. "I've always thought it ironical that we put the cross on jewelry. People were nailed to these things screaming in pain. Can you imagine having a huge nail smashed into your ankles! They died by the thousands of shock, loss of blood, drowning in their own fluids, and yet we nonchalantly wear it as though nothing horrible ever happened on it. It becomes nothing more than merchandise."

"I guess if nothing else the mind is great at denial."

A corner of his mouth rose in a knowing smile. "Sounds like you've accomplished that with Christianity."

I answered sincerely. "No, I wouldn't say denial. I've actually made a real effort to convince myself there is not just a loving god, but a god of any description."

"Convince yourself? That's a dead end approach to Christ. You aren't convinced that Jesus was God in human form. But you're searching for what Jesus may have been like as an older man so he could guide you and your friends in retirement." The professor was smiling at me like he saw a real disconnect here.

"Doesn't add up, does it?" I shook my head, sharing the professor's disbelief.

He stared at me knowingly. "I suspect you want badly to believe Jesus was divine. I suspect you're searching for a piece of reasoning that will give you a needed nudge to true belief. You're looking for a tipping point. You should have been in France in 1654 and met Blaise Pascal, a brilliant mathematician who suddenly turned his life toward Christ. He said, 'The heart has its reasons, which reason does not know.'"

I sat silently for a moment, realizing this man I had known for all of five minutes had hit on a quick truth. Maybe this was no casual hunt for ideas about retiring, but a far deeper search for where my soul stood on an issue I had grappled with for my whole adult life. Is there a god at all? Or is this pale blue dot of a planet, as Carl Sagan called it, filled with nothing more than pointless urging?

I could feel the gin warming my head. "I've heard a hundred times from my wife that reasoning is not the way to belief," I answered slowly as I was mulling over the quote. Not wanting to argue, I moved off of this uncomfortable examination of my motives. "Finding Christ would be an interesting by-product of my study, but for now my concern isn't the hereafter, it's the here and now." I was too intimidated after this exchange to tell him that in fact I was searching for a piece of proof of the Christ story that would be a game changer for me.

The professor continued. "I'm not even comfortable with that statement about the here and now. It's myopic and self-centered, short-term thinking in my opinion. But I've committed to sharing the Word with the unwashed," he grinned and looked pointedly, "so here are a few thoughts." I felt a subtle aggressiveness emerging from him. No doubt, alcohol brought him out of his timidity.

I had brought a legal pad and prepared to take notes.

"If you really want to know the fully human Jesus, you'll need to talk to more people than me. My area of focus as far as the historical Jesus goes is very narrow. It's limited to the early Jesus, his birth and the world he lived in as a child. It may have been very formative for him as a man. But obviously as a divinity he was not a product of an earthly environment."

"Since we're being frank," I warned, "I have very little interest in the baby in the manger story."

"Don't buy it, huh?"

"Nope. Well, maybe he was put in a manger, but the virgin birth thing..."

The professor shook his head and replied, "Oh boy, you're going to be a tough one. Don't worry, I'm skipping that part and getting into what may have formed the man, not the god, but the man. And it started with his birth, which is one of the most widely known events in human history. Every detail of it is a part of western culture. What is little discussed would have been the scorn Jesus would have received at being conceived out of wedlock, even though by the time he was born his parents had married. A woman getting pregnant, and not by the man she was betrothed to, and the subsequent child were both roundly, perhaps violently rejected in that very conservative Jewish society."

"I hadn't really thought about his neighbors thinking of him in that way. And I hadn't either."

"To Christians, to me, he was not illegitimate. Don't even think that word. He was conceived by God." He took a slow drink from the short, fat glass as though to reward himself for standing up for the sanctity of Jesus. He then noticed my glass had hardly been touched. "Have a sip," he urged cheerily.

To appease him and keep the conversation flowing, I lifted the glass and touched the gin to my lips, taking a shallow drink. "So you're saying he started life being condemned by people that knew him. Maybe that's why a lot of his story I remember is about his worrying over poor and sick people. Maybe he had been slammed his whole life, and it made him sensitive to people others looked down on."

The professor pressed his thin lips together in a pleased smile. "Very good," he said approvingly. "Very perceptive, and we are speculating only. I can imagine Jesus as a child catching hell—no pun intended—from other children; being seen as second class."

"If it was that bad, why didn't they move to another town?"

"They may have at some point. And I think it was the port city of Capernaum where Jesus gravitated to during his ministry. Early on he chose to give an interpretation of God's intent as he saw it in Nazareth. But interestingly in one gospel when he gave that reading of the Old Testament, his own townspeople tried to kill him."

"Shows you how little I know. Never heard of Caper...whatever." I admitted. "I thought Nazareth was where he always lived."

"He may have. I'm simply speculating and may be totally wrong. But my belief is that Jesus was humiliated verbally for all of his childhood. Being seen as conceived out of wedlock was just not acceptable. But that's speculation on my part." He was ever the academician striving for accuracy.

"No, it sounds plausible," I responded.

"So for your study, you might realize how searing and om-nipresent childhood wounds can be in forming who we become. I contend that these wounds are a reason Jesus the man, not the divinity, built his ministry around the humiliated, like lepers and prostitutes, and the poor. His message gave hope to those who had little of that. A subject he was personally and painfully aware of."

The professor turned his head toward the office's single window and stared at a large oak outside. "I would argue that his being defiant as a man and resilient in the face of constant criticism by priests were also a result of constantly having to defend himself as a child."

"So you're putting a lot of emphasis on his out-of-wedlock conception?" I had never thought beyond the manger story.

"Family honor, which meant the honor of the father, was the most cherished single aspect of that rural world. Getting pregnant before marriage was roundly scorned and probably no bigger insult to a prospective husband. So getting pregnant while you're betrothed to someone else was truly scandalous."

"Well, the story I grew up with was that Mary got pregnant by an angel or something like that."

He looked away from the window and at me. "And if the townspeople believed that, then my supposition that he grew up persecuted doesn't wash."

"You'd have to say Joseph was a pretty forgiving guy," I said.

He put both hands behind his head and stretched his chest outward in a deep breath. "Again, I sometimes try and put my own rationale around the Jesus mystery, but I wonder if Joseph wasn't the key to much of the Jesus human personality. You're right, for him to forgive and marry a wife he initially thought pregnant by someone else was a magnificent act of grace."

"So you can see Jesus finding out about the circumstances of his birth and being forever influenced by his father's ability to forgive unconditionally." I felt like I, for the first time in my life, was giving more than a passing thought to this man as a real live man.

"I still don't feel comfortable with this kind of speculation." The professor grimaced. "I feel I am being unfaithful to the divine Jesus and to the gospels. I reject imagining the mortal Jesus as being like any human influenced by his environment. But…" He finished his drink and reached in the drawer, pulling out the gin and pouring this time; he added no mixer. Without asking he leaned forward and poured a little more in my glass.

"But you are a curious, inquisitive human being. Are we supposed to be mindless to this faith? That's one thing I never liked about it." I said. "It seems there is no place for the individual."

He chuckled, "You would have made a wonderful Roman. They were very casual in their worship. They didn't like it when a god wouldn't answer a request they made for a favor. So they would curse the god's temple and refuse to take any more food offerings to them. I call them the-thing-to-do-believers, observing the religious festivals, because Roman society demanded it and friends all went. But they were wary of just how real their many gods were." He paused and asked with an annoyingly coy look, "Is that why you go to church? It's the thing to do?"

I ignored his snide remark. I didn't like this man and thought he was acting too familiar with me. "What about the Romans? What impact did they have on Jesus' childhood?" I asked.

"Oh, they were the bad guys. I call them ruthless economists. They conquered a country and let the rulers continue to run it. All they wanted was a continuous flow of taxes, crops, and they insisted on very strict order. Possibly Jesus had no grievous encounters with them early on. Still, he would have witnessed crucifixions in all of their horror. Certainly his exposure to the Romans would have been in the rebuilding of Galilee's largest city four miles down the road from Nazareth, called Sepphoris."

"Never heard of that."

"It was only four miles from Nazareth; may have had up to eighteen thousand people. Nazareth was just a village so insignificant it never appeared on a Roman map."

"How many lived in Nazareth?"

"Probably less than a hundred families. Built on a sloping hill with a spring at the bottom. Jesus would have easily seen Sepphoris in the near distance."

"I do know Jesus was a carpenter…"

"Maybe not in the strict sense of the word," he interrupted. "His father was probably as much a stonemason as he was a farmer. If Joseph found work, it would have been in the rebuilding of Sepphoris. There couldn't have been much need for a carpenter in a tiny village with mud and stone houses, mud-straw roofs and little furniture."

"So Jesus would have been a traveling construction worker because his father may have been the same." I had never thought about how much pure carpentry would have been generated in his hometown. I was quickly realizing how little I had thought about what kind of life Jesus the human led.

"Joseph disappears from the Jesus story after Jesus is twelve. I believe he died possibly during Jesus' early teenage years. Death came easy in those days. The average age may have been in the low 30's."

I was writing all of this down. "Why do you say Joseph may have died when Jesus was a teenager?"

"It was quite rare for a Jewish man not to marry, for a marriage was arranged by one's father. It is conceivable that a reason Jesus never married was that Joseph died before Jesus was, say sixteen, and a marriage could be arranged. I would also argue that Joseph could have been a man I would call a religious primitive."

"Primitive? Sounds like a hell fire and brimstone guy," I was giving observations just trying to stay in the flow.

"Maybe, but I mean Joseph could have been a back-to-basics Jew who thought the Jewish leaders were too wrapped up in their laws, and a young Jesus may have grown up listening to this conviction that God wanted a personal relationship with each of us, not through a temple's bureaucracy."

"So he could have both taught his son a trade, and set him on a path of rebelling against the Jewish establishment."

The professor chuckled and exclaimed with some glee, "Ah, the student has a quick imagination. Speaking of imagination, some think Jesus spent his twenties in India and came back a Buddhist. Or you could say he went to desolate northern Egypt where he was a hermit concentrating on prayer and disengagement from the material world."

The professor was obviously very loose now and enjoying himself and his comments. He twirled the ice in the drink, seeming to delight in the sound of the clattering cubes like a child playing with a yoyo or paddleball.

We had already covered twenty minutes, and my reluctant mentor rose from his chair and extended his hand across the desk to me.

"I'm sorry I have to stop our conversation so abruptly, but I've got 20 tests to grade, and I'm behind," he apologized.

I felt guilty about having taken up his time, but also felt I was just getting started in my questions. I hurriedly asked, "Doctor, can you guide me to some other experts on Jesus? As you can tell, I'm behind the curve on all of this."

He smiled knowingly, "Ah, the Lord works mysteriously. Especially on non-believers like you. Here, call this man. He's the head of archeology at Georgia State University. He's done a lot of digging in the Galilee region. He's even adopted part of the last name of the Egyptian Pharaoh Akhenaten III, King Tut's father." He handed me a piece of paper with the name Judah Akhen written on it.

"Oh, I almost forgot to ask you the reason I came here; what could Jesus have been doing if he had lived to 65?"

"You know I don't relish the idea of answering that." He shrugged as though he were apologizing.

"You believe fictionalizing the gospels demeans your faith. Right?" I asked of him.

"You know you are going to run into this with most theologians. Our professional and personal lives are foundationed on the truth of the Gospels, and we hold on tenaciously to the story of our savior as it is written. We dwell in the mystery of Christ, but we don't want to add to it."

I was frustrated and my voice announced it. "Do you hold on so tight because you are afraid your faith won't survive a questioning mind?"

He grinned as though he were enjoying my questioning his rationale. But this exchange could have easily turned into a confrontation. Who was I to come in off the street and challenge him about his area of expertise?

"That's a good rebuttal, my friend, but not accurate." He was like a boxer that had taken a punch to the face and didn't blink, then encouraged his opponent to take another shot.

"My journey to the truth has not been some casual endeavor. I have put a lifetime of study, questioning, doubting, and now being convicted of the truth of Christ as my savior. I have been through the struggle you may be having with what to believe. I have emerged not only with a great clarity, but a great respect for the story of Jesus."

"And I can appreciate that conviction." I surrendered to the strength of his commitment.

He stepped from behind his desk with the drink whirling in his hand. "Allow me to play psychiatrist. Architecture is a profession governed by the laws of physics. While your imagination is a key factor in designing a building, every structure must follow the law of gravity. Your design can't result in a building built on faith. So I would conclude you are a man of reason and rationale. Part of my role as a teacher of divinity students is to realize that some of them think that believing in Christ defies gravity, if you will. Still, I do think you're making a rather absurd approach to, not discover what Jesus would have done as an old man, but to discover if you believe in him as Christ. Because I suspect that's what's driving this."

Having upbraided me, he said, "Since I am, in part, about convincing doubters, I'll relent and venture a guess about how Jesus' life may have gone in later years." I had noticed his solemn reluctance to answer my questions and then he would find a rationale for going against what he said he stood for.

"Thank you for extending yourself. Again, this is just for myself and maybe a friend or two." I was wanly trying to convince him and myself that this absurdity, as he called it, wasn't going to get out and embarrass him.

"As an older man, Jesus may have focused more and more on the truly needy, especially on those rejected by most of society—lepers for sure; prostitutes and the crippled that begged. He would have remained a teacher by example. His service to the downtrodden would become legendary in his extended life."

"Sounds like Mother Theresa," I ventured.

His face then soured. "It's all one big disrespectful laugh to you."

I quickly tried to keep the conversation on track. "So in this scenario Jesus would have continued to give his love, but it wouldn't be through miracles if he wanted to survive the wrath of the Jewish leadership. Miracles would have caused too much attention."

The professor rattled the ice in his glass while thinking. "And then at some point he would have revived his aggressiveness against the Jewish rulers. He may have lain dormant for years doing solitary work without the disciples, who, after all, had to make a living."

I finished his thought, "So his ministry was not sustainable on a large scale. His business model, if you will, wouldn't work over a long period. If he did get aggressive again, he would have been killed."

"You've got it. And at a later age he still became our Christ." Dr. Gordon seemed comforted. But when he stood, his face went from a beatific peacefulness to a look of disdain, as though he were suddenly angry with himself for having ventured into a speculation that he had said he abhorred.

"But, Mr. McGrath, I doubt Jesus will ever be your Christ. You seem permanently fixed on the fence. This playing around with Jesus the man is trying to sneak in the backdoor to faith. Confront your reluctance. No guts, no glory."

He looked satisfied that he had washed away his guilt feeling, seeing me as the instigator of his going over a line he said he wouldn't cross. "Try Christ. Forget this Jesus the man nonsense."

That rudeness set me off and was compounded by the gin I had drunk and from which I could feel a definite buzz. And it was an angry buzz. I pushed my glass through the clutter on his desk and said as I turned to leave, "Jesus was called a drunkard, so I guess you're trying to be like Jesus. Have a tipsy day, professor." And I was out at the door, mad at myself for caving in so easily to the guy's demands that I take a drink.

I Was Somebody

I walked outside and stood on the main campus commons, a flat, grassy area of surprising clumpiness and dishevelment, where the grass is allowed the same independence as the students. Hardwoods tower over the area in solemn rows. There are few more sacred grounds to me than an aged campus necessarily anchored by massive trees with their trunks standing like enormous, twisting, sinewy arms caught in the act of bursting out of the earth.

I walked slowly toward the parking lot, a little tipsy, still a little angry, reconstructing what Professor Gordon had just told me. As I approached my car, a man and a woman with The Look saw me coming and walked toward me at once, both very focused on getting to me before I could open the door. The Look is that obvious run over, run down appearance that says louder than a neon sign, 'I'm homeless'.

Damn, have the hustlers come all the way out to Emory, I thought at the sight of them. Heat rushed up the back of my neck driven by anger so sudden I had no control over it.

Callie always cringed when we left a restaurant or the grocery only to be approached by a hustler in the parking lot. She feared my predictable explosive brush off.

Did they all go to the same tawdry tailor? Did they ever hear of a toothbrush? A novel idea, my cynical mind always thought, would be for the homeless shelters to teach them strategies on how to approach a potential donor. Is there no originality among the destitute? I asked Callie these questions one time and almost got slapped up side the head.

Why I do feel this way? I know I can be quick to accuse and be mean spirited. Maybe I'm too much an A Type. I see this man and woman with enough focus, target analysis, and energy to get out and beg where the money is, but not enough time to be looking for work.

Their faces were deeply wind and sun sculpted, alcohol puffed and acne cratered; all confusing just how old they might actually be. Unmistakable was the unwashed, tired, too-much-booze look that had become a stereotype, a cartoon, a photocopy of the last panhandler.

The woman stepped forward. The man stopped at my trunk. He looked Mexican underneath a soiled, low-pulled baseball cap. He wouldn't look at me, as though no eye contact rendered him invisible to my anger and rejection. He couldn't be assaulted by a bellicose man if he couldn't see the man.

She came forward without shame. She asked with the voice of a tortured throat, a throat ravaged by God knows what incendiary liquids and burning smoke. But her tone was almost bored, like this was a ritual; a perfunctory asking for bread, with the assumption none would be forthcoming.

"Excuse me, sir, we're hungry. Can you give us money for food?" I stared at her uneven teeth, which looked like a child had taken a brown crayon and marked on them. Her hair was a ragged, matted, undecided swirl of gray and blond.

The words boiled out of me at my resentment of this intrusion into my carefully planned world. "So you can go and buy some more cheap wine! The government is filled with food programs. I've already paid for you to eat with my taxes. How much more do you want?"

Her body fell back like my words had shoved her, like a hand or wind had slammed into her. She said in what I thought was a strange rebuttal, "Want? I served you. I was in the Army. I made sergeant."

"What's that got to do with anything? Obviously you should have stayed there!" I barked back at her.

She came to my door before I could shut it. "It was an honorable discharge. What about you? Did you serve? Have you ever served anything other than yourself?"

"What is this? You ask for my money and now you want to insult me? You should go to begging school, lady."

Her face had gone from indifference, a placid ask for help, to a fierceness. I looked in my rear view mirror to see if I was going to have to take on her husband too. He was leaning on my trunk, glaring at the both of us.

"Do you think we want to be here? I was successful. I drove a nice car. I'll bet I dressed as nice as your wife. I took my army money and put it all on running a delivery business. I was somebody one time. And I lost it all through a recession I didn't start."

This intelligent mind emerged like a moth coming out of a cocoon. She stood straighter, as though she were throwing off this persona of failure, this disguise, and morphing back into who she had once been. It calmed me down and made me more receptive to her plea. It made me feel guilty. She had been me.

The man had snapped out of his act of lethargy and was yelling in Spanish. I was actually thinking about reaching for my wallet and making a token gesture. It sounded like she was here by no fault of her own. But that outburst had me shutting the door and turning their moving mouths into soundless instruments. The moment was gone. I tapped the horn and he stepped to one side. She joined him and they left talking with great animation.

In the sanctuary of the car, I could feel my temper, my heart, my face screwed down and tight. I breathed in, trying to calm myself and feeling ridiculous at getting so upset.

Mine has been an anger formed by the virtue I see in accomplishment, smart decision making, and by trying. But that is a flawed assumption as the woman said. They tried accomplishment, and it kicked them in the teeth.

These encounters are swipes. We pass like two breezes going in opposite directions and touching only barely. It is an encounter without an appointment; a shock-entry into another's world. And who you are is not them. You almost don't hear their request because you're staring at their appearance in all of its portrayals of no. No dentist. No suntan oil. No barber. No clothing store. No saying no to a liquor store. No healthy food. No embarrassment at holding out a hand and asking you to fill it.

Our response is as stop-frame as their approach. In a second we say yes, and give them change, or join the chorus of no. No, I don't trust what you will do with my money. No, you are repulsive to look at. You are a canvas of economic and social failure on a hopeless slide forever downward.

As I turned out of Emory's gates, I saw them standing underneath a tree staring at me. Shadowed, silent witnesses to my rejection. Callie believes they may be God testing us. The more ruined teeth, sun-cracked face, unwashed matted hair, and ragged clothes, the more she thinks it is God testing. She believes God takes those that we would find most objectionable and pushes them pointedly at our comfort bubble to see if it will break.

Why have I been so judgmental? Whether they are buying the next beer or the next meal should not be my call to make according to Callie. She says you don't have to give until it hurts. Give until it feels good.

"Okay, okay," I said out loud in resignation as I looked back at them. "Next time I'll give you a couple of bucks. Go buy booze, dope, whatever it is you do with the money you lie to get." It would be servitude without a servant's heart; a gesture given for points on some celestial point list. Maybe I was starting to feel bad. But not bad enough that I stopped and fulfilled my promise of what I would do. Next time maybe. I had quickly and easily failed the Good Samaritan test. Again.

A Six-Foot Divot

Jack was a member of three of Atlanta's top country clubs. He invited our foursome to come as guests for a round at the Capital City Club. It's located in a picturesque residential area called Brookhaven. The clubhouse is a Tudor design that was once a large home. Its golf course flows along the soft undulating swells that give the area much of its character.

It was a clouding morning as I walked into the wood paneled men's grill. Jack, Max and Phil were already having coffee. Our tee time was 8:30, assuming the dew was off the greens.

"Hey, guys." I could feel the energy in my voice.

Phil looked up from a plate of sausage and eggs and said, "Cool it with the Mr. Happy routine. Nobody smiles this early."

I sat down. "I'm smiling all day, boys. We've just signed a nice contract to redesign an old county courthouse."

Phil looked disbelieving. "Nobody has business in this economy. Oh, excuse me, except government work."

Max changed the subject. "Listen, guys. I need your deposits for our Scotland trip. I'm thinking we'll hit five courses in six days. And right now I'm looking at October. But I've got a lot of people wanting to go."

Max planned a golf trek to an exclusive, to-die-for course every year. He had a list of over 40 men always ready to be invited, but he could only handle 25 per trip. He set up the hotels, transportation, and the tee times. He had made his living building houses, but his real passion was socializing.

I ordered a waffle, two eggs and link sausage. To hell with my cholesterol. "No wonder you're not building houses. You spend all your time planning these annual golf trips," I observed. How could he afford another $4,000, when his empty McMansions were sucking him dry with their loan payments?

"The day I don't have money for my golf trips is the day you put me in the ground," Max's words mumbled through his mouthful of pancakes.

I looked at Jack, whose face was noticeably saddened. "Jack, nobody likes to get up this early, but you don't have to be that depressed. We're going to dig up some divots in that Scottish turf, man. Let's get some excitement here."

He looked down at the table. His hands were twisting a paper napkin. Then he looked up with a sign of resignation. "This boy is going to be having some digging done, but it won't be by me, and it won't be in Scotland."

"Huh?" We all three exclaimed.

He took a deep breath and announced with some detachment, "Somebody is going to be digging a big divot. In fact, a six-foot deep divot and it'll be for me. I was told yesterday that I won't be available for a golf trip, unless you want to carry me in a coffin."

"Yeah, right," Phil scoffed. "Why would you say a dumb ass thing like that, especially while I'm eating a waffle?"

Jack moved his jaw slowly from side to side in contemplation. "I've not even told Betty. I met with a team of doctors at St Joseph's yesterday. I had melanoma four years ago. Had it removed with a pretty good cut. But now it's back and all over the place."

"Damn," I said softly. When we hear emotionally crushing news, news of a finality, we become bereft of words. Instead of a stream of eloquence, there is a singular 'damn!' or 'what' Or the even more inept, 'you've got to be kidding' and 'I'm so sorry', or 'oh, no'.

"Well, this can't be," Max refused. "Let's get some other opinions. You look healthy as a horse."

"No, I've already talked to several oncologists. It's all dooms-day for this lawyer. Got tumors on my kidneys and lungs. Too late to get 'em. Too many cancers. Everywhere."

Max stood up abruptly. "Well this is crap. Screw your doc-tor; we'll call what's that Anderson clinic in Texas or Mayo...or somebody."

I was surprised at how collected Jack seemed. It was like we were discussing some distant event, one of those earthquakes where so many people are killed that you are numbed to the toll and so just lay it out like, 'Well, that's life in China where that stuff happens'. Too distant to touch or be touched beyond the human, 'Gee, that's terrible. What's for supper, honey?'

Phil asked with incredulity, "Did I hear you say you haven't told your wife?"

For the first time his face flushed and his composure changed. "How do you tell your best friend with no warning that you're dy-ing in a few months? I'm telling you guys, because I need some words of wisdom here." Then the old Jack reappeared and he said, "Oh, sorry, using 'wisdom' and you three in the same breath is an oxymoron, isn't it?"

We all smiled weakly. Phil leaned forward with his elbows on the table. "Jack, this is no bull, right? You've been told that you're going to die soon. What is soon?"

He just nodded as though the words could not be ushered out on any amount of breath. The words were too excruciating to say, the despondency in uttering them so devastating. They had to stay suppressed or their issuance would wreck havoc on all of us.

A pause can have its own life; its own weight and feel; its own life form but one with its own stultifying darkness in which the mind stutters to a nonfunctioning stop. And then he said, "Soon. I mean not next week, but soon. This is the reality that doesn't seem real. When I was told I almost fainted. The terror was overwhelming. I could feel myself being crushed like you would crush up a piece of paper in your fist. My mind was so scrambled trying to process it, I guess, that I couldn't think clearly."

Max was solemn. "We gotta get some outside help. We need to call on The Man. Close your eyes and let's hold hands." Without pausing we held each other's hands while Max offered a short, impassioned, pleading prayer for The Lord to give Jack the words and the strength and the peace of mind to get through this. Max also asked Christ in particular to put his arms around Jack and to breathe fresh life into him. The four of us had never prayed together before.

"Thank you, Max," Jack said. "I don't know what I should be doing; running down the golf course screaming, cussing God, being excited about going to a heaven that I don't even know exists. This sounds stupid, but since I don't know what to do, let's do what we came here to do, hit some balls."

That seemed like a bad idea. I complained, "Golf? If you're dying, I think we can put that four hours to better use. We've got to save your butt. I think we should all get on the internet and try and find some specialist you can go to."

The others agreed, but Jack remained very calm and said, "Look, I've been getting weak over the past month and I don't know how fast this stuff is going to slow me down. Hitting some balls will get my head straight so I can talk with Betty. This is going to blow her away."

He stood up and said, "Our tee time is in ten minutes. Now get up and let's have some…" He started to say fun, but I guess it seemed way out of place, so his voice just dribbled off as he turned and headed toward the course.

We played to the ninth hole, having said little, making listless shots. The news wore on us and wore us down in eddies of emptiness, paralyzing sadness, confusion, and a fierce anger, each roiling over the other. As we walked off the ninth green I said, "This is crazy. What are we doing?"

Phil rammed his putter in his bag. "Yeah, this is crazy and it's unfair to Betty. Jack, you gotta man up and go home right now and tell her."

Looking distant, still in shock or utter disbelief, I suppose, Jack looked at the three of us and simply said, "Yeah."

I drove him to his car. We said nothing. What do you say?

He put his clubs in the trunk. I leaned out of the cart and said quietly, "Call me."

He pressed his lips firmly together, nodded, and we parted.

Son of a Pharaoh

Georgia State is Atlanta's big downtown university. It has no traditional campus, no grassy center with the big oaks that Emory does. But it has an enormous enrollment and a growing reputation.

The door had a small sign reading 'Diggers Do It Deeper'. It was opened and I entered a large room with broad flat tables around three of the walls. On each were cardboard dividers and boxes containing a myriad of clay bowls, some intact and others broken. Three blue-jeaned youngish people who looked like students were gluing pieces of pottery together and making notes.

At the far end of what must have been a forty-foot room, a thickset black man was bent over a table. I walked toward him, uncertain that he was the archeologist.

"Excuse me," I said to the man's back. "I'm looking for Doctor Akhen."

He straightened up and turned around, a striking picture of a man. His hair was black and straight and long. He had a tan tee shirt that fit tightly across his broad chest. It read 'When Negroes Were Kings'.

"Are you looking for the black or the white archeologist? Black or white?" He asked quickly.

I didn't know what to say. But since I could be as much of a wise ass as the next guy, I answered, "I never heard of a black archeologist."

"What about a Negro one. Ever heard of one of them?"

His voice was controlled, not as angry as his questions could imply. But I didn't know if he were kidding around, or what, so I said impertinently, "I never heard of a black archeologist who specializes in digging in Galilee, so I guess it isn't you I'm looking for."

His laugh was joyous and full. "I like that; a man unafraid to parry with his tongue. What a wonderful sword the tongue. I personally prefer the word *Negro*. It's more accurate than the hyphenated way to describe me." He stuck out a large hand. His palms were pink. His skin was so black it almost swallowed his features, a broad nose and broad mouth. "Welcome to the only place that's deader than downtown Atlanta on a Monday night."

I chuckled. "I'm a Buckhead Boy. Downtown Atlanta might as well be Mars to me."

"You people, don't you love that phrase 'you people', don't want to be around the beggars and the homeless. You don't like the down and outers. You like the up and comers. People don't pee on the sidewalk in Buckhead, do they?" He said words with a glee, like he relished them, and his enunciation was far more perfect than mine.

"I don't mean to be rough on a Buckhead Boy who seeks... what was it you were seeking?"

"I feel guilty taking up your time, but I'm trying to give some friends, and myself, advice about retiring. And we got to talking about what Jesus would have done had he lived to a retirement age. So you might say I'm seeking something stupid. What would Jesus have been doing at 65?"

His head nodded rapidly in agreement. He answered with a kind of quirky happiness that had me watching his theatrics, enjoying them actually, as much as I listened to what he said.

"Ah, the seeking. Don't we all love the seeking? And what is it you are journeying toward? What is its ultimate purpose? Is it really to find out whether to sit on your butt or not in retirement? Is it that mundane a search?"

His whole presence, the way he looked, gestured, talked, had rushed at me so that I was a little speechless.

I stared at him for a moment then defended our search. "We've got four fairly prominent men. One has a lot of money and plays golf all day. Another has just found out he's dying. And another is one of Atlanta's best-known homebuilders. These men could be doing something important regardless of how long they have to live."

"And what about you, Sonny?"

"I'm about to sell my architectural firm and am pretty clueless about what to do."

"So you seek a truth in an untruth that will make your lives more purposeful? The untruth being a 65-year-old Jesus. You seek reality out of fantasy."

I thought for a second. "You could say that. Yes, Jesus did not live long, so I'm seeking an answer that can only be explained through speculation. But an answer that may create its own reality through how we lead the last of our lives."

"That's rich. Creating reality and rationality out of something that never happened and, therefore is irrational, but then becomes rational." He seemed intellectually entertained.

"Couldn't you say that about Christianity?" he asked, carefully turning the clay pot in his hand. Colored on one side was a beautifully painted bird along with the writing he had been copying. "To the rational mind, could you say all religions are at their heart just speculation?"

"My wife would argue with you on that one. She is totally convinced that Jesus was Christ and is her Savior and that the God of the Bible loves her specifically."

"The writing on this jar was from a merchant writing praises to Herod's son Antipas. I found it while excavating Antipas' palace at Tiberias. The merchant is praising Antipas in hopes of getting a favor. It was all about self 2,000 years ago, as it is with you and me today. So don't feel bad."

I wanted to get on with my subject. "I told you I'm trying to learn more about what Jesus was like when he was alive so I can speculate with some feeling of accuracy about his possible later life. Dr. Gordon felt you had a particular angle on Jesus as a working man."

"Here, let's sit." He pulled up two canvas backed folding chairs. "I'll tell you that I am a Christian and an archeologist, a scientist. I have to speculate often in my digs, but I like to feel a certain certainty about my religion. Now, of course, religion is ultimately an act of faith, which is probably the first cousin of speculation."

I interrupted him, "But you have to speculate. We all do constantly. I had faith or speculation that I would drive safely over here. I had no ironclad assurance I would arrive without a wreck. So I don't see that speculating on any subject is inherently wrong."

"Agreed," Judah concurred. "I do think faith is a stronger level of conviction than speculating. I want the fact that I have given much of my heart and mind to Jesus as Christ to be a commitment that is based on as much fact as I can accrue. I don't want to be guiding my life around something that in fact is not a fact. And once I settled on Christ as my Savior, I don't want to start nitpicking that commitment to death wondering if this or that is really true."

"Is that why you are an archeologist in the Holy Land? You are trying to find fact by digging into places alluded to in the Bible and proving they really existed? Are you trying to prove the Jesus story?" I ended with a soft laugh, not wanting to sound like I was accusing him of doubting his faith.

"Very good. A little questioning of my commitment," he responded with some eagerness. "But not entirely true. I was an archeologist long before I became a follower of Christ. The Mediterranean seacoast has always been my area of work. I became intensely interested in Jesus while on a dig at the port city of Caesarea and within a year became a follower."

"In the nitty gritty of everyday life, if we traveled back and saw him, say at work, what would be our impression?"

"Excuse me, Judah," a thin, casually dressed young man approached us from a cubicle. "National Geographic is on the phone." And he handed Judah a cell phone.

Judah nodded to me, pointed toward the phone, and said, "Hello, Robert, how does our application look?"

It was a brief call, with Judah doing a lot of nodding and a final, "Well, I know you are pushing it for us. Be in touch, my friend."

He folded the phone, pressing his lips together in a discernible frustration. "Our application for a grant to dig is under final consideration, but the competition is fierce. Everybody wants a *National Geo* grant to pay for their own excavations."

"So this school doesn't pay?"

"Colleges today are strapped to pay their light bills let alone pay for a dig in the ground 5,000 miles away. Money is the fuel that drives archeology and the tank is low in this economy. We really need private benefactors right now."

He was quiet for a moment, absorbing the less than satisfying call, then returned to the subject. "I immodestly am considered an expert on life in Palestine 2,000 years ago. But I cannot tell you factually what Jesus looked exactly like or what he was doing in his twenties before the Gospels pick up his story.

"Paul writes in Philippians, 'Jesus made himself of no reputation, taking the form of a servant, and coming in the likeness of men.' And Paul wrote that 'Jesus humbled himself and became obedient to the point of death'."

"That says Jesus looked like a man, but why didn't the Gospels describe his appearance or reveal more about him on a human level?"

He twisted in his chair and crossed his legs. "The Gospels weren't transcribed at a Jesus speech, though persons now unknown may have written his sayings soon after he died. But the book of Mark wasn't written until after 70 AD, maybe 40 years after Jesus' death. The other three gospels dribbled out over the next 10 to 30 years."

"Are you saying none of these four actually heard Jesus speak, nor did they write down what he said as he said it?"

"If you had heard Jesus speak and you were so impressed that you wanted to write it down, why would you wait 40 years to push out to the public what you had written? Now that doesn't mean that a man now known as Mark didn't hear first hand, had a great memory, but didn't feel the need to formally write and present his writing until later. It is believed that someone, not Mark or the others, was the first writer. Mark copied the mystery source's work, added what he might have remembered from hearing Jesus first hand, and also wrote what others who had been there said they heard."

"I didn't know there might have been an original transcriber whose name is unknown," I said.

"Actually, I doubt Jesus' words and his story were written down during his short ministry at all but were memorized. Not many of the common people could write. There was a whole class called scribes, and I doubt any of them would be following an unknown wandering teacher."

I was perplexed. "But if the first gospel wasn't written down until 35 years later, how could anybody remember all of that?"

Judah laughed. "It was a very different world from ours. Most people were illiterate. Papyrus was too expensive except for government and legal documents. Animal skins and little wooden tablets with wax on them were the preferred things for writing on. So people knew what they knew through memorizing. And they had extraordinary memories by our standards."

Judah then caught himself and said. "Actually, Paul wrote his letters way before the Gospels, maybe twenty years earlier. So someone may have written down the Jesus sayings soon after he died," he continued. "But I would wager Jesus' sayings were based for the most part on either the memory of the writers, a bright and attentive follower, or the disciples."

"Why wait until Jesus was dead before writing it down?" I asked.

"His significance was not fully realized until his death. You see, there were many street preachers roaming the roads, many magicians, healers; a real menagerie of characters claiming closeness with God. Some of what Jesus was doing was fairly common. How he did it by building a self-sustaining organization, and what he said were very uncommon."

"But didn't he attract thousands of people? Surely someone seeing those crowds would have thought he was more important than the average preacher. I always thought Jesus dominated the landscape with everybody talking about him."

He shook his head. "There may have been a few thousand at a handful of his teachings; certainly there was real intensity at many of his healings, but in the larger scheme of life in Palestine, his ministry was short and didn't touch that many while he lived. Look at who was with him at his death, only his mother and another woman, which makes it even more remarkable that we're sitting here talking about him."

I yearned for the personal stuff. A facial description or personality trait. "You're saying that only what Jesus said, out of all of those other preachers, was remembered. So what he was saying and when he said it impressed the stuff out of somebody. I do wish they had written more personal information."

He reached on the low table next to us and absently turned a piece of broken pottery in his fingers. "Just give me the facts, ma'am. Height, weight, color of eyes. Lay the facts on me, or I ain't buying." He shook his head in amusement.

"Those who wrote the Gospels were not writing them as a biography but to capture this unique message. They had no use for what he looked like or specific personal quirks or even if he were married."

"So given that there is nothing specific about what he was doing in his twenties, what do you think he was doing?"

"That's an area I feel free to speculate on, because, as you say, the Gospels say nothing about those early years.

The first thing that would surprise you if you saw Jesus would have been his small size and the shape of his face."

"In all of the paintings I have seen Jesus is a lanky, long-robed, English-looking man with shoulder-length hair," I said.

Judah shook his head. "Wrong. My team dug up the partial skeleton of a man in his twenties from the first century. He was five foot four. His skull showed him to have a square face. Jesus was not the Jesus of the paintings. He was shorter in statue. His hair may have been longish, but not to his shoulders. He had tanned, olive skin. No white man to be found. Sorry about that, Buckhead Boy."

"That appearance would be weird. I'd wager it could even shake the faith of many Americans. The Jesus of our paintings is a European Jesus, not a short, square-headed man." I literally could feel a slight disappointment at the thought of this strange looking figure that countered my life-long image of him.

Judah stood and yelled, "Little man, you ain't my Lord! My Jesus is a six-footer and practically white." He did a little dance jig and sang poetically, "My Jesus ain't small. He's tall. And to my delight, my Jesus is white."

I laughed at his carryings on. "So what kind of work; what would he have been doing?"

Judah picked up a cloth, squirted a clear solution on it and began rubbing the crust off what looked like a fishhook. He held it up to me. "This tells much of the untold Jesus years to me."

"A fish hook?" I asked, confused.

"Jesus may have been a stonemason and a wooden scaffold builder by trade, but I believe he was a fisherman in his heart. You see, Herod's son Antipas had been appointed as the ruler of the Galilee area. He also inherited his father's penchant for building elaborate palaces, temples and buildings that looked like they were right out of Rome.

So not only was he restoring Sepphoris right down the road from Nazareth, but he was building a great port and a palace for himself on the Sea of Galilee. He named it Tiberias after the emperor Tiberius."

"So you're going to say Jesus took his tools and worked in the building of the docks or maybe even on the palace."

"Well, think about it. If Jesus were a carpenter and he lived 15 miles inland from the sea, why were none of his disciples carpenters? Why were so many of his stories about fishing? He always seemed to be around water. He even walked on it for goodness sake!"

Mentally I was scratching my head. "Hadn't thought of that. But I've only been a skimmer of the Jesus story, a little here, a little there. Certainly, no in-depth knowledge."

"You're like a lot of Christians, most of whom have not delved into Jesus as a human. They read the Gospels, for the reasons they were written: to have his messages revealed, to learn how to live their lives."

"That and it's hard to figure how he could have been both God and a human." I said with some confusion. "And we want to read the God part because that part can benefit us, can save our rear ends for eternity. It can answer our prayers and erase that big eating cancer or get us a job. What can the human do for me?"

Judah shouted and his laughter washed the room. "Lord, he sees the light. This seeker has dug deeper than I have and has discovered more than I ever will."

He looked at me, grinning, and said knowingly, "Only a really self-centered man could have made that astute self-analysis. You yourself have never had any interest in Jesus the man, other than you've always heard he was the only perfect, sin-free human."

"And I never related to a perfect person. He always seemed abstract. Not really human." I agreed.

"Oh! No!" Judah yelled. "You don't call slamming money tables all over the Temple acting human? You don't think getting angry with his disciples, even calling Peter the Devil, and calling the priests hypocrites isn't being a real man? You don't say these are the actions of a tempestuous, impassioned human? No, this was Jesus as a true man, not some abstract God."

Why did I feel like a child being scolded? "Yeah, I read those parts, but it didn't register. The perfect man branding overrides everything."

He leaned into me from his chair like the force of his presence would imprison me. "And it never registered, to use your word, when Jesus was sweating blood out of sheer terror before being arrested, that this wasn't a human being just like you?"

"I guess it never registered, because, again, the main thing I remember about Jesus was that he was perfect. His sweating on a hot day, stubbing his toe, getting mad and blasting his followers, that part has never registered."

"Now that you have a real live, sweating human being in your sights, allow my imagination to continue. As you know, well, you don't know, but Luke 2 said, 'Jesus grew in body and spirit, living in favor with God and others.' So he was developing both as a human and in his spirituality, which sounds like a regular person growing up."

He looked at me intently. "Let's be honest here. You don't know me and will probably never see me again. So tell me, you don't believe in Jesus as the Son of God, do you? And secondly, you really don't believe the god of any religion exists, do you?"

It was so abrupt and confrontational, such a change in the roll of the conversation, that I felt my face turning red as my mind raced around his words looking for an answer. After some very sluggish seconds I answered with resignation, "No, I don't, is the most honest answer, but I hold on by my mental fingernails to some hope, some faint belief that it is in fact all true." I was again denying the existence of the God I had been raised to believe in.

He rested back with a look of satisfaction. He then startled me and the students working nearby by announcing as if he were at ringside announcing a fight, "Let the world know that Mr. Sonny here does not believe there is purpose in this life!"

"Damn! Do you have to tell the world?" I shot back, feeling like some dark family secret had been revealed.

"Oh, so now you're feeling a little embarrassed. Maybe your friends will hear the announcement. Maybe one of them is walking past the window right now and he'll run tell everyone that Sonny thinks God is a joke, a myth, for the empty heads, the superstitious." His eyes were wide in some kind of wild joy at having found a man, me, who was living a lie.

I started for a moment to get up, tell him to kiss my butt and leave, but that would have been a coward's way out of an accusation that happened to be true. I wanted to get off me, who apparently had been outed for believing this is a world without purpose. So I tried to get back on subject.

"I thought you dug in the dirt, not in people's minds. Let's move away from me and back to the man you say I don't believe in."

Judah grinned broadly, pleased, for some reason, in his ability to discover the hidden.

"Okay, Okay. So Jesus would have had to work. And I believe Jesus may have worked in the rebuilding of nearby Sepphoris; perhaps working alongside Joseph while he was still alive. Jesus learned the stone and wood working trades there. Sepphoris had its own Buckhead in a way, a wealthy enclave mostly of Jews. You should see some of the floors that have been excavated. Really beautiful and expensive tile art."

Judah continued, "In my imagining of Jesus I would say work started over at Tiberias in 20 AD as work winds down at Sepphoris. His father is probably dead by then and since there was no construction work around Nazareth, he moved out to work on the port. I believe that here he met his band of brothers, fishermen like Peter and Andrew."

"One of the facts of Jesus' life that I never gave much thought to was his walking along the Sea of Galilee, seeing some fisherman and saying, 'Follow me'. I mean they didn't appear to know him. But then he was Jesus, so maybe he was one of those people who have the 'It' factor and we are automatically attracted to them."

"Jesus Christ superstar. I think you are dead on with that observation. Fishing was tightly controlled by the Romans and local tax collectors. You had to have a license and they didn't just hand them out. Peter and his brother Andrew were businessmen, owning their own eight-man boat. I have always had trouble with that story myself."

"So you think Jesus met Peter while working in the port city. Is this correct?"

"I repeat, my friend, this is rank speculation. For all I know he was never a carpenter, but studied the Torah all his life."

"Okay, now that you've qualified what you're saying to be without empirical knowledge, what do you imagine happened next?" I was feeling the immediate collegiality that I'm sure everyone who met Judah felt for him.

"I imagine Jesus met Peter and Andrew and their circle of friends and built a strong bond with them. I believe that his friends recognized him as a very holy, very intelligent man. I can see them already marveling at his knowledge of the five books of Moses and the intensity of his relationship with God."

Judah shifted in his seat and continued. "When John the Baptist exploded on the scene, they knew Jesus was going down to see him. In my imagination, when Jesus returned, they saw perhaps an extraordinary intensity in him, yet a serenity that was palpable. He must have also developed his message, which had its own appeal. It obviously was so mesmerizing that Peter was agreeable to either shutting down his fishing business, which is unlikely, or turned it over to a trusted friend."

I could see the face of Judah's watch and realized I was about to be late to meet a client. "Judah Akhen, son of a pharaoh, I have to leave this enlightening trip to the past and go back to work. You are so kind to afford me this time. But I must ask you the question that brought me here."

"Yes, what was the question again that pushed your sails in my direction? Ah, yes, to find Jesus the Elder, I believe."

I nodded in agreement. "I know this would change the story as we all know it, but we're acknowledging that it never did and never could have happened. Now that I have all the qualifiers, Doctor, what might Jesus have done with a longer life had he been crucified at 65?"

He smiled, knowing I was trying to relieve him of his distaste for rewriting scripture. "Good job. I would first say that Pilate would have released him. This would have elevated Jesus, humiliating the Sanhedrin leaders and forced them to back off going after Jesus for a bit.

I believe he was still severely beaten before being let go. Jesus would have gone through a long recovery in a secret house in Jerusalem, being too badly beaten to travel. When he recovered, he would have gone back to Capernaum where Peter lived."

"So his ministry would have stopped for a while so he could recover, which calmed things down." I suggested.

Judah stretched his legs out in front of him. "You know he died very quickly on the cross. Many who were crucified lived for two, even three, unimaginable days. I think Jesus was so badly beaten he died from that and not just from being crucified. Being 'hung from a tree', the phrase they used for being crucified, obviously brought on his death. So had he survived the beating, it would have been a long recovery."

"You say he may have gone to Peter's hometown, but Peter denied him. Even I remember that. To do this he would have to forgive Peter for that betrayal, plus the rest of the disciples, which to me, were a pretty gutless group."

"Oh, that's a little harsh," Judah protested. "These men gave their lives for him later, so don't be too hard on them. Look, they thought Jesus was the Messiah, but then there he is lying on the ground beaten to a pulp and dead. Talking about betrayed; they probably felt they were the ones let down."

"Good point."

Judah continued, "My older Jesus goes to live in either the small port town of Bethsaida or close by to that in the port village of Capernaum. Matthew 4 says after Jesus heard that The Baptist had been put in prison, 'he went and lived in Capernaum.' So he already knew the town. In an act that symbolizes unbelievable grace and forgiveness, Jesus forgives his disciples for running out on him. Especially Judas and Peter."

"To forgive the unforgivable would have gained him more notoriety and validated his message as being true and pure." I surmised.

"It would have given him even more credibility. I think he might have spent the additional 30 years developing disciples. But they had to come to him. He couldn't be roaming the countryside as he had before, pulling in more believers. He would have created a teaching, training, and mission ministry out of the northern Galilee, into Syria possibly, but far away from the hotheads in Jerusalem. In one of his most famous instructions in Matthew 28 he had told his followers 'to go and make disciples of all the nations'. So my older Jesus would have fulfilled his own commandment."

"I think in business terms you're saying that his model for running his business had already caused his death. Wasn't he repeating the same dangerous way to market his ideas about God in that scenario all over again?"

"No. In this story Jesus the Elder would no longer travel in his own country. He would not go into Jerusalem again to confront the priests. And he might have told his new recruits to leave Palestine and go into other countries."

"So, how does this story help my retiring friends?" I inquired.

"You said these men were all successful. That means they didn't do it alone. That means they probably had many helpers and friends, disciples, along the way. Successful people like to be around successful people."

"So you're going to say they should gather friends or others of similar interest and push a cause. They should create disciples for their cause in retirement."

"I would suggest, whatever their passion, that they carve out an amended version of what they had been doing before. They could start a whole new cause or expand on a cause they have already supported."

"Use their leadership skills to lead," I summed up.

"I like that," Judah said as he touched my elbow and we started walking slowly to the door.

"We didn't get around to your namesake, The Pharaoh. I would like to do that sometime."

As we got to the door, he reached onto a desk for a piece of paper and a pen and scribbled down a name. "Here, call this woman. She's an astrophysicist, evolutionist, philanthropist, and very keen on discovering more about Jesus, though she doubts he was Christ.

She has her own spirituality, an extraordinary student of life. Tell her The Pharaoh sent you." He gave one of his infectious, rolling laughs and turned back into the room filled with moments written on clay shards and molded into pots and hand lanterns; snippets of the lives of others that fired the mind of Judah.

I left feeling I had now publicly denied that the life of Jesus had any eternal meaning by denying he was more than a man. While I felt embarrassed for some reason when Judah shouted it out, I also felt freed. I was free from my childhood of saying 'Yes' because my parents, my friends, my culture, said I was not being good unless I believed. I was now free to confront a world with no purpose or morality except what I wanted it to have. But I was also free to find that there was meaning to it all. My dear Callie would have said that I am a scrambled egg of a man.

Looking for a Parachute

Where did July go? Time was on a tear. And then it was August and the sun felt as though it had made an angry descent closer to the earth. Atlanta is a heat island; though canopied in trees, its asphalt lays its hot hand open and each parking lot is its own stovetop.

The Creeks Country Club golf course is just outside the reaches of Atlanta proper, but still simmers over its grassy expanse. In August you have early tee times. You want to be off the course and under the constant winds of cooled air inside the clubhouse by lunch.

We met at the grill at 7:30. Jack came in with an almost brazen smile. He walked tall and erect as he approached our table. Max was eating breakfast and Phil and I had just ordered. When we eat, we don't wait for the others to arrive. You get there. You order. You eat. Stragglers are not accorded civilities.

But as he sat, Jack's face looked as though he had taken the flat side of a piece of white chalk and scrapped its powder over his cheeks.

"Today I own the course. We're talking all fairways and greens," he announced with too much bravado.

Phil had a link sausage in his fingers and was eyeing it and turning it like it was a piece of fine jewelry. He seemed to ignore Jack. "This is life. The essence of all that is good—a perfectly cooked, cardiac-arresting, grease-dripping sausage. I eat this sausage as a way to prove my manhood. This is a death-defying act as surely as charging a hill in wartime."

Max's bass-sized mouth was filled with eggs, which didn't hinder his talk muffling through and over them. "Phil, haven't you read? You're behind the times. America is being feminized. We don't need real men and their testosterone anymore. Who are we going to beat up? The end of the warrior is here. So don't play manly man with that damn sausage. We're supposed to share our thoughts with one another, and, oh, by the way, no one wins or loses on the course today. That might hurt the feelings of the one that loses."

I was still focused on Jack and his over-the-top behavior and paled-out face. "Jack, if you could understand Max through that half dozen eggs he's eating at once, he says we're supposed to be girly-men on the links, which means you can't *beat* us today, you have to sha-ur your score so we come out equal," I said.

Jack smiled agreeably.

Phil had been watching Jack's almost erratic behavior and asked, "What's with the Mr. Happy Face? You haven't heard some news that's going to have us all grinning, are you?"

"The damn cancer's in remission, isn't it? Time is back on your side." Max exclaimed.

Jack kept smiling, but it looked forced and frozen.

"Friends, time is on none of our sides. As hard as we run to outrace it, it still wins. Only I at this table know when my race will be over."

The three of us, feeling elated and hopeful, quickly felt our spirits draining.

"And that means..." I asked reluctantly.

"Got the news yesterday. Today is August first, and I may not make it until September. The stuff has really spread; all systems are starting to shut down as we sit here."

"Damn," we all said collectively and with that sinking, pulling down, heavy force that rides in on news that upends lives and breaks life's normal course.

"Thank you for your solemn salutes," Jack said. "I've chosen to end this with a smile. I refuse to go 'screaming into the night', as Eugene O'Neill wrote. But since the three of you don't read anything outside the sports pages, you never heard of that book."

"You know, Jack, all doctors aren't the same. You always hear about one that's figured out a new treatment that the others don't know about. Have you gone on the web and called around? Surely there's a way out." I said.

"Oh, I could take some heavy duty chemo, and then I might get a month or two. But that's a torture chamber."

His grin had faded. His face was stoic. "No, there's no way out, but I'll have to ask, as the firing squad loads its guns, and as the wings fall off the plane at 30,000 feet, is there any way in?"

He was looking at me, and I asked, "In? In what?"

"Into heaven, or some second life. Aren't you messing around with finding out about Jesus? I'm looking for a parachute into that place I've been hearing about in church all my life."

"I'm starting to cool down on that old Jesus thing. Everybody I interview reminds me of how stupid this subject is and how ignorant I am about it."

"Well, get stupid, and get going. I need somebody as lost as I am to show me the way out."

"Jack, it was a crazy idea to start with. I'm not trying to prove Jesus existed. I'm looking for some ideas on how to retire. It'll take a while," I answered defensively.

Jack pressed his lips together, cocked an eyebrow at me and said, "I don't have a while."

We all said our now patented, unoriginal 'damn' in unison.

Max had exhausted his breakfast. He pushed the empty plate away and agreed, "Yeah, four weeks is not a while if it's your last four weeks."

I felt I was being put in an unfair position. "Jack, this isn't some serious search. I'm just knocking around imagining what Jesus the man would have been like. It was just some idle talk on the golf course. Knowing some facts about Jesus the man isn't going to get you into anybody's heaven."

His teeth clinched in resignation. I didn't want to know the darkness he was looking into. He was reaching for straws, for a life preserver. 'No' was not an answer to this drowning man. But why was he looking to me to discover a path out of the looming darkness of his being?

He answered, "Yeah, you're right. You're one of the last people somebody would go to if they needed their soul saved."

Whoa. That hurt, even for a doubter like me. I'm clinging on to more belief than I realized or his assertion wouldn't have rocked me like it did. He knows I want to believe there is a God, but 'want' doesn't work. I'm no guru anybody would turn to for The Final Answer.

Jack continued. "It's just that I don't relate to what I call religious people. I guess I thought since you were about as heathen as I am, if you could find Jesus, then there must really be a Christ attached to the end of his name. You may be the last one to call for help, but you're my last life preserver. And I'm calling."

"Well, thanks a lot, best friend," Max said indignantly. "I'm the go-to guy at this table about Christ. You should be asking me about our Lord, not this lost soul, Sonny boy."

I quickly took advantage of that offer. "You're right, Jack. Max is the foursome's full-bore believer. He might even be able to slap you upside the head, yell 'Heal!' and you fall over backwards a new man."

Jack sat back in his chair as the waiter delivered his link sausage and eggs. He looked at the eggs and said ruefully, "I haven't ordered this plate of grease in years, but damn if I'm not going to eat every shred." He looked up and with a semblance of a grin said, "Ah, the freedom of knowing you are about to die. Drink yourself stupid. Clog your arteries at every meal. Live the good life until there is no life."

"Sounds like a good philosophy to me," said Phil.

"Is healthy eating and exercise a joke?" I asked rhetorically. "You've been on vitamin supplements, soy this and soy that. Hell, you won't even eat barbecue."

Phil said sardonically, "No wonder you're dying. A man's gotta eat pig burnt over an open fire, or his maleness disappears."

Max glared at Phil. "You are the definition of stupid. Our man Jack got that melanoma playing golf. Golf in the sun is what's killing our boy."

Phil agreed. "Golf has killed everybody that's ever played it."

"Enough of this crap," I interjected. "Jack, I'll move quicker on this Jesus thing if it's important to you. But if you're looking for a Jesus parachute, you need to see a minister."

Jack had lost his happy patina. His face had an anger about it. "Those guys speak in platitudes. It's a canned mimicry filled with clichés. No, save me from the preachers. I feel more comfortable having a guide that's lost, a man in search of his own parachute."

Max grumped. "Well, you've got your man with Sonny boy. What we have here is the blind leading the blind toward a place neither one believes exists."

I was losing my bearings over this good friend's life, now on an uncompromising clock. Jack had always been a rock to me. But he was no more of a rock than any of us. What pathetic little globs of chemicals we are; a night light's worth of electricity; a trillion cells all pumping in blind unison, driven by this absurdity called a life force. What a joke it all is. But I now had no choice. I could no longer say these things; have these thoughts; feel disdain about the absurdity of it all. My dear friend sought, desperately reached out to, meaning and a way to continue life in another form. But what a lousy guide he had selected.

"Okay, Jackster. I'll push this, whatever this is, along. I'll see if I can find some answers, but you know what a skeptic I am. I might suggest you take up Hinduism, or maybe nothing. Maybe this is all a big fat nothing."

I could see Jack's face falter. He didn't want to hear the word *nothing.* "Surely there's something," he said meekly.

I shook my head. "Jack, we're big boys here. First of all, I really don't know where to go to find an answer as profound as the one you want. Secondly, I'm going to be straight up with you. If after a few more interviews I feel like I do right now about religion, I'll say it ain't so."

It was obvious Jack was keeping his sanity by holding tightly to his hope that the day after he died would be filled with light and life; another and more glorious life under somebody's religion. He was hoping for Christianity since he had given his money and time to that one.

"Oh, you'll find a positive answer, I'm sure," he said cheerily. It hid his desperation. The man did not want to die and be dead. But who does?

Phil said dryly, "This conversation is absurd. Since men could think, they've been trying to figure out the meaning of life; brilliant people, great philosophers, and still it's up for grabs. There's thousands of books on the subject, and you expect this architect in a few weeks to figure out the most perplexing question ever posed? This is nuts!"

Jack said quickly, "Yeah, nuts is good. He's my man. He's hungry like me for some truth. He's a skeptic, a man of reason, not overly intellectual; a common-sense man. He'll journey out there and get me an answer." There was a sprig of confidence in his voice that actually buoyed me.

"No man in this grill wants to be in this grill a month from now more than I do. My sweet wife and the children are crushed over this. They all sit around the house crying. I'm living for them now more than for myself. I would at least like to go out believing I would see them again. Somewhere, some how." Jack said.

"So you're saying dying sucks." Phil tried to bring some levity into this heartbreaking scene.

Jack gave a breathy laugh. "Wait until it happens, boys. Max, pray all those eggs you're eating drop you like a rock so you're dead before you hit the floor. Who wants a couple of months of this withering away, knowing it's coming on?"

Max was picking his teeth with his fork. "Hey, thanks, heathen. But the difference between you and me is that I have no fear. I've given my life to Christ and when He's ready, then I'm ready. I'm free from fear. You're frozen by it."

Phil leaned forward on the table with his elbows. "You know the great characteristic of humans? We are all deniers. Bad wrecks, floods, being hit by lightning, big eating cancer, dying; all that happens to somebody else. I think having a well developed ability to deny is the way to human happiness."

"What's this, a new philosophy for guiding our lives?" I responded sarcastically.

"No, I'm serious," Phil pulled a golf tee out of his pocket and unconsciously started fidgeting around with it. "How do you stay sane if you accept all the misery that exists on the planet? And then one day after bad things happen to other people, it happens to you.

The phone rings. The doctor says you'd better come in; I've got the test results. So you start grabbing for hope and in grabbing you're ignoring some awful truth."

Max screwed his cavernous mouth up and said, "Ignore? Isn't that the first part of the word ignorant? Or ignoramus? Which is what you are. Damn atheist. Our buddy Jack is looking for a life preserver that will float him into the next world, and the skinny one here is offering no hope except hope for the moment."

Since much of our relationships was built around insulting each other, Phil ignored half of what Max had said. "Get real, Max. There is no other world. I know it's heartbreaking, but I would be a liar to a dear friend if I suddenly started praying for Jack. I offer honesty to my friend. It's an honesty filled with the tragedy that is life. It ends. There are no escape routes."

"Alright, listen." I had been eating and listening and saw the conversation was getting absurd, like we usually carry on, a mind-less blithering, kidding, insulting. "Jack, if you refuse to go to a preacher and you won't let Max help, as I said, I'll keep looking for the smartest people I can find. But no promises."

Jack gave an honest appraisal. "I know now what it's like to be run over by a truck, and I know the pain it causes your loved ones who witness it. I appreciate each of you, and what each of you has said. I know you want to help. But apparently there is no stopping this stuff, and I'm just seeking peace of mind so I don't go screaming down the street in stark terror."

Max stood up and announced, "We've all got to man up on this. Today we will make the course a sacred place. Jack, you ride in my cart. You may not can hit 'em anymore, but you can watch a master."

"A master of what?" Jack grinned. "Eating a tuna fish sand-wich in one gulp?"

With false bravado we all walked slowly from the grill, arms on one another's shoulders as though we were going into battle, which emotionally we were. And I didn't feel comfortable we would win. This enemy was unmerciful.

You're Doing What!

Callie was on heaven's stairway everyday, involved in a women's spiritual mentoring program and a group leader at a well-attended women's Bible study. She read scripture every morning and before going to bed. Her faith was better tended, I would think periodically, than our marriage. She called it a journey of joy. She asked that I join her. I told her I would tag along behind while I worked my mind through it.

Over dinner that evening I announced "I've now had two meetings with two doctors."

Her eyes widened in fear. "What doctors! What's wrong? Why haven't you told me you're sick?"

I had to laugh and reached out to her hand to calm her down. "No, no. Not a medical doctor; a doctor of theology and of archeology. You know the old Jesus thing, about retirement. I can't believe I found somebody to talk to."

She then asked with obvious curiosity, "Sonny, we've gone to church for our entire marriage, but we both know deep down that you go half because of me and half because you get to visit friends. So what's with this sudden interest in Jesus? I mean, I think it's wonderful, but, honey, it's, let's say, very unusual. I guess my first reaction, and I hate to say it, is there must be some self-serving reason and not out of a love for Christ."

"Excuse me, while I take the knife out. I could counter that little jab by asking this: isn't trying to get to heaven self serving? Is this all really about pleasing some unseen God, or is it about people wanting to live forever on some fantasy island called Heaven?"

I could see a small explosion coming so I quickly continued. "I've told you how this got started. It was just a lark. Okay, a stupid lark. But it's gotten bigger for me than Jesus as an old man. It's made me start thinking about Sonny as an old man. Which on the one hand is depressing as hell, but on the other hand it's forced some urgency into what I'm going to do with the rest of my life."

I loved the way she put food in her mouth. It was a subtle slide into a barely opened mouth; so genteel; so ladylike.

She calmly changed the subject. "Didn't you all play golf this morning? How is Jack?"

Knowing she would be shocked, I said as softly as I could, as though that would reduce the impact, "Not good. Jack told us that he might not live to September."

"What! That's four weeks. Betty didn't tell me. I saw her at the grocery store and she didn't say that. I told her our prayer group had a prayer chain going."

"Well, it ain't working. Apparently it's spreading fast and now is all over his body."

We both sat quietly and ate our food mechanically. We were imprisoned by our disbelief. I finally said with no energy, "You'll love this; Jack wants me to be a messenger."

"A messenger? What kind of a messenger? What message?" She was confused.

"He wants me to tell him if there is a way out."

Callie mouth contorted as though she were about to scream. "He wants you to help him commit suicide?"

I almost laughed, but she looked too aghast. "No. He wants me, of all people, to see if there's a parachute available. Is there really a God in some religion, hopefully the one he's put a lot money into. If I tell him I think some religion or force is out there, he can, well, make peace, get on the right side, have some hope that he would be a candidate for a life after this one."

Callie slammed her fork onto the table with a declarative force. "A parachute! A candidate! Jack spends his entire life deny-ing Christ and now when it serves his purposes, he wants Christ to suddenly step in and say, 'Oh, Okay, Jack, you've rejected me all of your life. Now when you want your butt saved you call on me, but only for your own selfish reasons.'"

"Well, listen to the big Christian. She condemns those who don't have a perfect church attendance record or can't just accept a faith because all their friends say they should, which means there's no room in the inn for this dying man who has done nothing but good things all his life for people." Why does the intensity level of anger rise in proportion to the level of love for one? It wasn't hate or disdain, but sheer, old-fashioned mad I felt toward what I saw as her religious elitism.

"And just why did Jack ask you to discover if there is a heav-en? How dumb is it to go searching for something you don't even believe exists?" She was incredulous.

"That's why he asked me. I don't know whether I believe it or not," I admitted. "He felt if I could get one inch of insight into whether there is any meaning...if I who am so unsure could find some reason for this world, then he would leave this life with some comfort that there was more life to be had."

Callie shook her head with an obvious anger. "What am I missing here? This whole idea is like the theater of the absurd. I have truly married an idiot."

She loudly started clearing the table as though she had to do something, anything other than throw dishes at me. Anger re-quires its own action. She stopped in the kitchen door, plates in hand, and said with all the control she could gather at the moment, "Giving grace to late believers doesn't mean Jesus is gullible. Whatever analyzing, deduction, mathematical equations or interviews you do, it comes down to faith. You and Jack have got to give up this proving your way to heaven nonsense."

"I love these fights over the man of peace," I said sardonically. "Isn't that the story of this religion?"

A shattering explanation mark, with all of its implied profanities, exploded out of the kitchen. Never has a plate thrown into a sink so defiantly ended a conversation. I quietly left the dining room for the safety and solitude of the den. Jack's soul, along with mine, already resided in Hell, as far she was concerned.

One Tough Cookie

After my time with Judah Akhen, I was behind on putting together drawings for the old courthouse in Covington we had been asked to redesign. Very early the next day, Tuesday, I was walking into my office when the company phone rang.

"McGrath Designs," I answered.

"Ah, the sinners do rise early, don't they?" It was the always joking, slightly high-pitched voice of my Senior Pastor Sandy Rutherford.

"Sandy. It's a little early to be saving sinners, isn't it?" I kidded him.

"God's messenger never sleeps, brother. I'm scouring for sinners twenty-four hours a day," And he laughed his short, punchy laugh.

"Listen, Sonny, I want you to buy me lunch today and for that favor I will grant you a favor. I want to make you an offer you can't refuse. An offer, if excepted, will give you at least half a chance of making it to heaven's door." He was always dealing, a master manipulator and cajoler, especially when it came to raising money for the church.

"Yeah, the door is about as far as I'll get."

Sanford Rutherford has led Dogwood Presbyterian, one of Atlanta's 'big steeple' churches for 20 years. He was hands on and all out; a pastor in ever sense of the word. He worked the church halls during the week like a politician running for office, slapping backs, squeezing forearms, laughing, calling all he met by name.

Lunch was his time to work those from whom he needed fellow-ship or funds. And he did it by parceling out tidbits of supposedly confidential information about city leaders or some plan he had for the church that only the lunch companions thought they were privy to. He was short in height and round in body. Behind his back he was known as Friar Tuck, because of his jocular nature and his appearance, especially in his Sunday robe.

The restaurant Stones is synonymous with steak, which means men; which means dark wood walls, soft lighting, and a feeling you are among those in the know and those you should know.

Sandy was eagerly greeted by the maitre de and two waiters, both who knew that the guest paying for Sandy's lunch would never short them on a tip in front of this master of Atlanta's spiritual universe.

We had hardly placed our orders before his demeanor went from teasing and angling for any information to serious. "Our church has a real need at this moment for smart leadership. I'll tell this to you, and it's not for public consumption yet."

Uh, oh, here it comes. He sets me up with a my-ears-only revelation.

"We have a narrow window of opportunity to buy the apartment complex across the street from the church, and I need the strong backing of men in the church like you, whom a lot of people know and respect."

I took a slow drink of water, wondering if my pocket was about to be picked. "Why would we want to go into the apartment rental business?"

"Two reasons. It's a safe place to put some extra church money. And that property is in foreclosure. We may want to build a youth center or a Christian school over there some day. If a church isn't growing, it's dying."

I knew he was studying my every blink and skin twitch. Reluctantly, fearfully, I asked the exact question I knew he wanted to hear, "How can I help you?"

One could argue against a proposal too strongly and never be asked to buy his lunch again, and being ousted from his power circle of confidants. I didn't say so, but both our church and its soaring budget had gotten too big for me. Only Sandy's unique and loving pasturing kept me there.

"You're going to come on the session and be an elder. That way you can work hand in hand with me and other leaders." He was trying to give some monumental importance to his request by painting it with his most serious, official stare.

Being a church elder was the last thing I wanted to do. The 50-member group supposedly governed the church. New members were to go through a vetting process by an elder selection committee. In fact, candidates were selected by Sandy, who told the committee whom he wanted. He stacked the session so that it basically followed his wishes.

I thought I would protest anyway. "The committee won't vote for another month, and none of them have called me."

He waved his hand as though the committee was a fly he was shooing away. "No, the vote has been taken on some early members. You're in."

Right. "So what's a new member have to do; just show up?"

"You stand in front of the other elders and tell about the joy you had when Christ first came into your life. It can get pretty moving."

I panicked. That moment had never arrived for me. What in the world was I going to say? I couldn't lie. I vainly tried to get him to reconsider. I said with a big grin, "Well, Sandy, if you want me to talk about a joyous moment, it would have been in the Chi Phi fraternity basement at Georgia. We had a black band called

The Hot Nuts that was singing bathroom-wall songs. I had my arm around this drop-dead, good looking girl, a Budweiser in one hand, and I can still remember that being a moment of pure joy."

His face screwed up in pain and he begged, "Lord, save this sinner. I don't think I would tell that story! But you were young and foolish. I want your mature man story on the joy you've found in Christ."

"Aw, you know I'm pulling your leg. I'll be good." I was lying. My story was true. That night, now thirty-five years ago, was pure joy swimming in lust and promise and anticipation, and the thrill of standing next to one of the school's most desirable gifts from The Lord. I thought as Sandy and I ate lunch that I had never felt joy of any kind in religion, and felt sick even thinking about telling a bald-faced lie in God's house in front of 50 of God's best.

After lunch we returned to his office at the church. I had told him at lunch that I was researching Jesus the man for some retirement thoughts. Sandy had a national reputation for his study and knowledge of the humanity of Jesus.

He sat in a cushioned rocking chair, always close to his visitor, and sitting back in it as though his visitor made him feel relaxed. He deeply loved people and it showed. He made a steeple out of touching his fingers and said. "A few thoughts: I've got a funeral here in an hour and a wedding an hour after that. The end and the beginning, all in one hour, all very human. Just like Jesus was, as human as you and I."

"How do you deal with those emotional swings?" I asked.

"It's all God's work. He wants us welcomed into this world, and he wants us welcomed again into his world in heaven. I'm just officiating at both homecomings."

Nobody could give a homespun answer like Sandy. He had a way of cushioning and celebrating life's ups and downs.

"Sandy, you'll think I'm nuts, but I've gotten intrigued about the notion of Jesus having lived another 30 years, and living into his 60's."

He smiled impishly, "Well, that is nuts, but, hey, you're an out-of-the-box thinker, so that's the kind of question I would expect from you."

"Don't think I'm being sacrilegious; just wondering if an older Jesus could give me some insight into how to live life in later years." I was feeling him out to see if he found even the discussion of a delayed crucifixion offensive.

His thin lips contorted in a perplexed way before answering me. "Honestly, it does bother me a little, but then again not so much that I don't find it intriguing. And maybe I'm willing to discuss it, because I suspect it's you trying to find faith in ways that only you can." He was too perceptive.

"Okay, so let's talk about Jesus the man. You're well known as a student of the historical Jesus. Give me your take on the man and not as the divinity."

Sandy answered quickly, as though the subject was at the top of his mind. "There is a paradox about Jesus the working man. On the one hand he may have been a traveling craftsman, skilled in stonework and carpentry, and yet he proved to be a brilliant teacher, quick with concise rebuttals, and with a detailed knowledge of what we now call part of the Old Testament. The skill of a laborer required little intellect; the other skill, a teacher, showed him to have a soaring intellect, accompanied by charismatic presentation abilities."

I spoke a thought I immediately had. "If I had been an architect back then, I would have hired him according to how exacting he was in fitting wood and cutting stone. He would have to have known how to make mud brick, cut and dress wood, as well as chisel stone. He would necessarily have been of substantial physical endurance and strength. I agree, it doesn't add up that such an intellect would have been basically a construction worker."

"Exactly," Sandy agreed with a grin and said, "Now that's a daunting thought; having Jesus apply for a job with you and you didn't know he was actually Christ."

He continued, "Jesus had another unusual quality and that was that he could read, as so many were illiterate then. Also, he probably knew three languages."

"I thought he spoke, what was, it begins with an A?"

"Aramaic. Yes, that was the common language of the people of Galilee. He taught in that. Since he was quoted as reading the Old Testament in the Nazareth synagogue, he knew Hebrew too. But the English of the day was Greek. If he worked in Sepphoris or Tiberias, he would have spoken Greek. If he couldn't read, he had one whale of a memory."

A brilliant mind, a holy man, and a traveling construction worker. Sandy was right; it didn't add up. "Maybe he never was a carpenter. Maybe he spent his twenties thinking, studying, and molding the man he would be. Maybe he went back to Eqypt, living like a monk." I conjectured.

"I don't think so. Men worked back then. There were no welfare programs like today. I think he was doing both; working in some capacity, maybe even working as a fisherman on Peter's boat, while growing in his passionate pursuit of the more perfect man at one with God. No Temple, no priests, no laws necessary. No family or tribe or town loyalty. No material lusts. No dreams of treasure. Pure man. Adam again. One to one with God."

"And I suppose the whole love thing, that was his main message." I said clumsily.

Sandy rocked back and shook his large, baldhead. "The 'love thing'! And I've asked you to be an elder? The love thing was at the heart of his ministry. Love for God. Love for one's neighbor. Love was the foundation for forgiveness and grace."

"The church does not need this illiterate on the session, Sandy. I just don't know this stuff." I was being completely honest.

He played me like a cat plays with a mouse, just for the fun of it. Rolling his eyes heavenly, he scoffed, "Stuff! You call our faith 'stuff'? I have to be a forgiving soul around you, brother, so let's move back to our imagining."

Sandy rocked slightly as he talked, a reflection of the boundless energy he seemed to possess. "Jesus spoke very economically and in punchy, provocative statements. His great intellect allowed him to immediately answer those who challenged his knowledge of the Jewish Laws. You just try coming up with a rebuttal that is presented in a parable. Dream it up on the spot. That requires a level of mental dexterity that I can't fathom."

"Okay," I admitted, "this is where I sound real stupid. What exactly is a parable and why did he use them to argue or teach?"

"You're concerned about looking stupid? You mean more than you already have?" He loved it, but only because we had become good friends over the years, which in my and his world meant affection was shown through bantering back and forth.

"In a mostly illiterate society, learning was done through memorization. The most effective way to have someone remember teaching was through story telling. But the story needed to grab the listener's attention and make them think. Parables did that. They stuck in the mind. They were very short stories, almost one-liners, about some everyday event, but with a moral or spiritual message as its true meaning. And Jesus spiced his up with a shock value. Some were outlandish and made listeners think through the meaning."

Sandy absentmindedly rubbed his corpulent stomach that rose like a mound.

"My grandmother told us stories every night when we were little. My parents told us some. But I don't remember telling my children stories that had been passed along to me," I remarked.

"And you can track that lessening of the importance of story telling with the rise of literacy and technology. Why tell your child a story you made up when they can read books, or watch endless stories on television? I consider it a great loss." He genuinely seemed hurt.

"What's with his helping lepers and prostitutes?" I quizzed him.

"One of his great personality traits was extreme sensitivity, especially for a man, to the pain and suffering of others. It was like the plight of others was almost unbearable to him as a human." Sandy paused, contemplating what he had just said, possibly because Sandy himself worried so greatly and so obviously over his own flock.

"Israel was a class society in a way. One didn't help those outside their family, community, or close friends like we do today. And men stayed well away from women except for their wives. Jesus broke a lot of cultural rules, especially in his reaching out to women. He truly hurt for the helpless. He was in agony for the downtrodden. A level of selfless service unheard of at that time became one of his great characteristics. I believe he hurt so deeply for others that it would have sent us into deep depression."

"You say he went against his own culture, which took some kind of courage. You say he was sensitive. I would say he was a radical and one tough cookie."

"Forgive him, Father." Sandy gave a mock prayer. "Do we need to call our Lord and Savior a cookie, even a tough one?"

I shrugged, "Okay, one brave man."

I had left my notebook in the car, so I found myself continually trying to summarize what I was being told. Sandy was right; people today can't remember jack. Especially me.

"See if I have this right. Jesus was intellectually overqualified to be a construction worker, which he may never have really been. He could have lived much of his 20's around the Sea of Galilee, around fishermen. For a man of the times, he was seen as too sensitive; he hurt too much for others. And he was an unparalleled storyteller."

Sandy seemed pleased. "I'll say you may actually be getting a feel for the man. Perhaps a miracle will be performed and you'll get a feeling for the man as Christ."

His eyebrow went up and he stared at me like a parent coaching a child. Sandy and I had never discussed religion in the ten years of my being a member of his church and on a friendship basis for most of that time. He was a locker room kind of guy, in the cut-up fashion of men teasing men. I told him once he should carry a towel around so he could snap everybody he passed, then snicker in that devilish grin he easily displayed.

Sandy rocked for a moment, then said, "One of the shocking things Jesus did, and even more courageous, was to step outside the strict boundaries of loyalty to father and family. His 'love everybody' idea was unheard of. You cared about your father first, then the rest of your family, not the beggar in the next town."

"Your father was your resume," I offered.

"Exactly. It was who you were to yourself and the rest of the world. There was almost no upward mobility as far as having a better job than your father. You pretty much learned his trade and did what he did."

"I can see why the poor stayed poor and the rich got richer. A very static economic world."

"Which is what the Romans and the few wealthy wanted. There was little innovation or invention, because designing a laborsaving device might put people out of work. Jesus' concern was with the soul not the job market, but having said that I will say his message was a reflection of how the Jewish mind was being impacted by the economics of the day."

"Jesus the economist. The man could do it all."

"I'll have to give you credit; that feeble joke has some truth. Jesus was a master communicator. He talked to the times. His message of hope, his constant references to wealth envy, and of a kingdom that was both here now and coming, may have addressed the impact of Herod Antipas' rebuilding of Sepphoris and the construction of Tiberias. In fact, Sepphoris was called the 'Pearl of Galilee'."

Sandy patted a book on his desk. He had to be moving some part of his body, it seemed. "The Romans knew that big temples, amphitheaters, and palaces intimidated the masses and reflected power. Antipas created a gleaming city on a hill that was straight out of Italy. Jesus could have stood on the slopes of Nazareth and easily seen the white marble from four miles away. The revitalized Roman administrative center attracted many wealthy Jews and others who made their living as merchants, lawyers, and land owners."

"Sounds like I could have made a good living there as an architect," I conjectured.

"If you were Antipas' main architect, then maybe so. But artisans like architects were often looked down on by the wealthy because they worked with their hands; therefore, seen as just another common laborer. Sculptors, artists; creative people didn't get the credit for their work. The rich guy that paid them got all the credit." Sandy got up and took a stack of mail from his secretary who came in without knocking. But such was the informality of his ministry.

"It's hard to believe the people who designed those fabulous palaces and amphitheaters weren't honored like today's designers. The design of a multi-mile aqueduct alone was amazingly precise in weight loads and the delicate fall of the water shoot." I know I sounded dismayed over this lack of ancient respect.

Sandy thumbed through the stack of letters and printed advertisements as he talked. Looking down then up at me, he commented, "The result of these two wealthy cities in the middle of poor subsistence farmers could have resulted in two economic events that guided how Jesus talked to the people. One was the turning of small farms through both legal and shady means into large estates. This made a former small landowner an employee of a wealthy man, more aware than ever of their poverty and more envious of the wealthy."

"Do people ever change?" I laughed. "Sounds like today."

"I think human nature has not changed an inch since humans created what people considered to be wealth. Maybe that is what is the meaning of the Garden of Eden and the loss of innocence." Sandy observed.

"Anyway, what also may have happened in Jesus' day, as a result of these wealthy cities in the middle of relatively poor farmers, was the dislocation of the family unit," he said.

"That sounds boring; no offense." I apologized, but this sounded like we were getting into a class on sociology.

"Well, to a heathen wantabe like you, no offence," he winked. "The breaking up of the foundation of Galilean society, the family identity, their sense of place, the loss of their all-important house, could have dramatically affected the way Jesus presented his story of salvation.

"If vineyard people, sheep herdsman and farmers were displaced by losing their land, then their family might have to split up and move into the cities to survive. This broke the inheritance lines and sons doing the work of their fathers. And it broke their connection to the place they lived. The poor landless farmer became dependent on the big landowner or Herod, and not on his family. If this occurred, it is a major event in the time of Jesus."

"So how might this factor into how Jesus talked?" I asked.

"His message was pretty radical. He said love of God was more important than love of family. He said forget about material possessions. It was actually a message of hope for those who had lost hope in the new Galilean economy. And his statements about the place you would live in wasn't your old house, but in the kingdom of God. This sounded like a caring, loving, new world was awaiting the faithful. And it addressed the issue of the destruction of the family."

"I can see why Jesus said the pursuit and envy of wealth was its own devil and its own god. I see that every day at the club. I see it in myself." I observed.

"Jesus was unequivocal and unrelenting. He was laying down a restructuring of the Jewish faith, which stripped it of its obsession with a complex array of laws and made worship very singular. He said God was the new Father, not your earthly father, and the farm, your family land, was irrelevant; that you would live in God's kingdom. These were shockers. They broke the bonds of family and home, but at the same time made this break okay."

I shook my head. "Sandy, I'm starting to add layers on to this oversimplified version of an antiseptic Jesus I have always had. My new descriptive adjectives would be iconoclastic; astute observer of the human mind and the times; an iconoclast with a singular focus, and again, one tough cookie."

Sandy's assistant appeared in the doorway and pointed at her wristwatch. He gave a little salute to her announcement that he had an appointment. "Okay, my friend, let's wrap this up."

"In view of all you have just shared with me, and it is a lot, and I thank you, what would my imaginary Jesus be doing had he lived to 65?" I repeated what was becoming my mantra.

We both stood up and he clasped my arm as we turned toward the door. He was in his early 60's but still with the thick shoulders and neck from his years as a boxer in college and the Navy. But his girth had rounded away what must have been a muscled body.

"I believe he could have started a new version of Judaism. But it wouldn't have been called that. The Jewish faith was already a fractured grouping of interpretations of the books of Moses, and they co-existed with some comity. It was a big tent faith. The ultra-conservative Essenes headquartered on the Dead Sea; the Pharisees, strict adherers to the Laws; and the politically active Sanhedrin constituted the primary divisions. So Judaism had long ago divided along various interpretative line." Sandy summarized.

"Jesus' doctrine, based on hope, love and God's grace, would not have been called Christianity. His rising from the dead is what resulted in his version of Judaism really taking off and being called Christianity. So some awkward name like esusites may have emerged as his brand." I conjectured.

"Not bad, brother." Sandy said. I was holding him up and wanted to go, but was caught in the web of this conversation.

He continued. "Jesus could have emerged, not as a pacific teacher in a small town, but as a religious leader who established a major center for his new version of Judaism. In this scenario, he would have been highly successful. He would have been head-quartered somewhere in Galilee. There would have been no second Temple. Probably just a large compound like the Essene sect had out at the Dead Sea at Qumran. He had already proven himself a remarkably organized leader."

As we got to the door, he had this small moment, as he did to all of his men friends. Looking me in the eye he said, "You know I love you, brother, and so does Christ." There was an awkward-ness in it, as men, the one's I know, don't often say the love word to men friends, but it was touching and bonding, and it was part of his persona that made him so beloved and so powerful. He loved deeply and he needed love awfully.

"Sonny, I know you struggle with faith." He looked at me with some sternness. "Know that I haven't spent my life promoting a lie. The story is true. Trust me."

Distant Dreams

A Picasso exhibit was in town, and Callie and I were invited to a fundraiser based on his art at The High Museum, Atlanta's temple to the painter and sculptor. On a slight grassy rise above the omnipresent Peachtree Street, The High is a stark white, simply designed plea for a rabid sports town to drop its football and baseball for an instant and sophisticate its soul with works of creativity. For the party I had my penguin-best tuxedo. Why not ask everyone to donate the money they spent on hairstyles, jewelry, and clothes and come in blue jeans? That savings alone would beat what was about to be donated.

Callie had complained about coming. 'That crowd', she now called the group she once flitted with, was now too vapid in their conversation. She said they laughed too intensely, an interesting observation of a nuance I thought. All they ask about is whether you've had any parties up at your lake house at Burton, or how the beach has been at the condo at St. Simons, and at which med school Taylor or Megan had been accepted.

It's easy to cast a cynic's eye on the accomplished. If I do, I cast it on myself, because I am comfortable being a fish in these waters.

We walked down the long spiral walkway that hugs the museum's wall and where the crowd below can be seen as you descend. Callie stopped and held me back with her hand on my arm.

"Why don't you quiet everyone down, and I'll make an announcement?" Kidding was a constant between us and one of the strengths of our marriage, so I was already grinning.

"Mark 10:21. Read it, brothers and sisters," she said in an uncomfortably loud voice as we stood now only a few feet above several hundred people.

"Hey!" I exclaimed in surprise. "What the heck is that about?"

She looked serenely at me, confident in her words. "It is the most difficult, the most shattering advice to us and this group that Jesus ever gave."

"And what was that?"

"Go sell everything you have and give to the poor, and you will have treasure in heaven."

"Oh, please. My wife has become a Jesus freak," I said in exasperation.

"Not a freak, a follower," she rebutted confidently.

"Honey, these are our friends. We have been on boards and held fundraisers with them. Without their 'everything' you deride, there would be no charities. Where's the money coming from to help the poor? Not the poor, that's for sure."

I wasn't angry. Just frustrated with what to me was becoming over the top allegiance to Christianity. I even saw it as becoming a threat to our marriage. I was digging in against religion or maybe it was her persistence; what to me was her growing obsession about it.

Several women's voices rang out above the din of chatter.

"Callie! Down here." As they waved, they motioned for us to walk the last few feet and into the crowd.

Taking my cue from her friends and wishing to escape from this religious conversation, I nudged Callie into the crush of conversation, packed bodies and jostled drinks.

"It's the A couple," JuJu Sherwin yelled in her bullhorn voice. It was a shrillness that could be heard over the most raucous cocktail party.

We worked our way next to her and her husband Jeff, the human version of a keg. He loved a good time, as evidenced by the fact he was holding a wine glass in one hand, a beer in the other.

JuJu was a sorority sister of Callie's. A surprisingly large number of their class of Kappa Gammas had remained in touch. They had formed a potent force when they all joined Atlanta's Junior League in their late twenties. They called their click The KG's, and they had muscled money out of the Delta's and Coca Cola's and Georgia Power's of Atlanta for years, not to mention many insurance-wealthy widows, for the League's charities.

Jeff laid his thick arm on my shoulder. His grin pushed his cheeks into reddened tennis balls. "Hey, congrats, my man. I heard you were selling your firm. Who'd you sell it to, Obama?"

"Yeah," I kidded back. "If they can buy into General Motors, why not a mom and pop architectural firm?"

"Since you're on speaking terms with the President, how about getting him to force the banks to refinance twenty-five of my two million dollar condos that are sitting empty. Hell, I'll let him move in one for free."

Jeff, the newspapers said, had eight mill of his own money in a 36 story, beautifully built tower. The 25 condos were to start at two mill. After a year he had sold two of the units and was facing foreclosure on the entire building. Real estate has always been Atlanta's primary product, but it was now a product that few wanted. It was an unfolding tragedy, rippling out to architects, builders, and all of the plumbers and electricians who put these buildings together. It was an angry, accelerating wave, carrying all ships that rode its waters to a very rocky shore.

"Well, sorority sister, I hear you are practically running your church now." SuSu's voice was as loud as the utter whiteness of her perfectly altered teeth.

I knew that kind of comment, though said facetiously, was embarrassing to Callie. She was a leader of several committees, but was too modest to admit it.

"Oh, I'm just trying to earn forgiveness for our wine and roses days at Georgia." She tried to laugh off the compliment.

Every pore of SuSu's face grinned and flushed red. "I do remember the wine, but I don't remember getting any roses. Don't you just hate it that we can't raise hell anymore?"

Callie smiled and said with some force, having to elevate her otherwise soft voice, "No, I already did that. I'm trying to raise heaven now. Does that make sense?" She screwed her face up in a silly questioning look.

"Oh, Callie, you're just getting soooo religious on us," SuSu moaned, still showing teeth.

Jeff leaned in and giggled, "I think you could use a double shot of Jesus, SuSu. You may be too close to the Devil."

SuSu pushed against his thickness, "Well I sure got close to the Devil when I married you." And they both laughed heartily.

Knowing Callie was ready to move on I said, "I hate to bust up this Kappa meeting, but we need a drink of this high priced wine I'm paying for."

Jeff held his wine glass up and proclaimed. "It ain't high priced in taste."

Laughs take the place of words and nods. They're like punctuation at the end of a sentence, whether the remark was really funny or not. And we all laughed at Jeff and using it as a wave of the hand, Callie and I leaned against the throng and headed for a bar at one end of the cavernous gallery.

At the bar she saw two more girlfriends. I nodded to her that I knew she wanted to talk to them and gave her a little 'see ya' wave and turned to see Mickey Sams, a lawyer I've used before, talking to a tallish, athletic-looking woman in a beautifully tailored beige blouse and white pants.

Mickey saw me and motioned for me to come over to meet his friend. Her hair was uncertain in its mix of blond and slight gray streaks and fell easily over her broad shoulders. I guessed she was in her early 50's. Confidence exuded out of her as easy as her breath.

"Sonny McGrath, meet Sharon Gold," Mickey said as we exchanged pleasantries and shook hands. She had a capturing face; tanned, creased, but not severely, with large brown eyes. She had a wide, thin-lipped mouth colored with a glossy, pink lipstick. Her name resonated with me, as I vaguely remembered Judah recommending I see a woman with a similar name. Maybe it was she.

Introducing us, Mickey said, "Sonny's architectural firm does the design work on restoring old warehouses and courthouses. And Sharon is a student of the stars, she told me, otherwise known as an astrophysicist. But she just said she was going to underwrite a dig in Israel. So sounds like you're both into old stuff."

"Maybe it's because I am old stuff," I responded.

"I too have followed time's arrow obediently," she acknowledged.

"Sonny, you may have visited the ancient Egyptian art exhibit that's down the hall. Sharon, or the Gold Foundation, made that possible. Her husband was an incredibly generous man to this museum and its galleries. You might say he was high on The High."

"I did read about the exhibit and about your husband. I'm sorry about his passing." Jonah Gold had made a fortune with several high profile, class action lawsuits. He had retired at age 50 and then became one of Atlanta's great philanthropists until his death several years ago. But I was unaware of Sharon, his second wife.

"Oops," Mickey said suddenly as he looked down at his Blackberry. "There's a nighttime jury decision coming in on a case my firm has put a lot of effort into. Now that ya'll are new best friends, I've got to get down to the courthouse." He nodded at us and melted into the crowd.

There was an awkward moment where we both looked a little forlornly after our fleeing friend, not knowing if one of us would say 'hey' to a friend and disappear. But I was fascinated by both her work and her sponsoring a dig. I also found her whole demeanor appealing.

"This sounds stupid," my words stumbled out, "but you remind me of Aspen, Colorado."

"I didn't know there was an Aspen look, so I don't know if I should be insulted and walk away or be flattered." She sounded coy.

Then I didn't know where to go with such a sophomoric remark. "I've skied there many times, and maybe it's my imagination, but I have this look I always associate with men and women I've seen working there. By the way, it's a compliment." *Hey, you're flirting. Cool it,* I thought.

I changed the subject. "Listen, I'm fascinated by your job. Cosmology and all things to do with the birth and evolution of the universe have fed my imagination since I could read."

She took a sip of her chardonnay. "People think of outer space in the context of Star Wars and The Alien; movies that don't seek an intellectual understanding of our universe, but they use space as a backdrop for exploding space ships and scary creatures."

"Ah, the unappreciated scientist. But it is interesting that you make your living studying the heavens, but provide funding to digging in the dirt."

"I think on my tombstone I want written 'A Student of the Order of Stuff.' I like to study how and why things work. I make my living being curious. Kind of neat."

"So what's this dig about in Israel? What's that got to do with finding order in this chaos called the universe?"

"Would you mind if we sit?" Sharon asked. There was a cushioned marble bench against the wall and just away from the crowd. The noise level was a degree lower, but at least we didn't have to shout.

As we sat down, Sharon said, "I have found contentment in how mathematics is the language of how the universe works. But I have no answers for how we humans find peace in the chaos of our existence. My husband was a devout Jew, but he married an agnostic: me. Recently, I have become interested in the life of Jesus and his breakout emphasis on the individual and on an orderly world based on love. Still I am today not a true Christian, but one on an intellectual pilgrimage to first find out just what kind of a man he might have been."

I assume my mouth dropped a little. She saw my surprise.

"An agnostic being interested in Jesus doesn't warrant that kind of look, does it?" She chided with a half smile.

"No, no it isn't that. It's just that I've got a personal study or search going on about Jesus the man, and to hear someone I would just bump into say they had that interest, well, yeah, it surprised me."

She was so easy to talk to that I confessed, "I left religion when I reached puberty. Didn't set foot in a church from 13 to 32, when we had children."

"Me too, kind of; I pretty much dumped religion in college. I was rejecting everything, much to my parents' anguish. I had a love for science, and especially physics. I found a comfort in the certainty of logic and mathematics. I actually found more wonder and beauty in science. Religion seemed to me like an attempt to give meaning to life."

I was about to respond when I saw Callie coming toward us. She had a smooth, economical walk. Her face was small as were her well-placed features. Her eyes were an intense blue that were almost distracting when you spoke with her. She was walking a little briskly, like she was in a hurry to go some place else.

"Glad you came over," I greeted her. "Callie, this is Sharon Gold. My wife Callie."

"Well, I certainly know of your foundation and its good work. So nice to meet you." No one was more gracious than Callie.

"Thank you. I appreciate that," Sharon answered.

"Honey, you won't believe this. Sharon was telling me about an interest she has about Jesus the man, and a dig she is sponsoring in Israel."

Callie said with a laughing voice, "Better watch out or he'll be sending you an application to grab a trowel and go over there."

"Yes, Sonny said he was studying, or searching, for information about Jesus the man. It's pretty ironical; two people with that particular interest would meet here."

Callie looked knowingly. "God works in mysterious ways, they say. Sonny is trying to prove his way to heaven. If you're further along on the journey, perhaps you can help him."

I lumbered into that comment with a response that Callie always thought absurd. "She's right. People talk about making a leap of faith. I'm building a bridge of facts that will lead me unequivocally to heaven's door."

Callie said, "Men. They have to be in control. Can't let go and let God. Actually, I came over to ask a favor, Sonny. Three of my sorority sisters are here, and we all want to go out for a drink and some quiet chitchat. Would you mind if I left and saw you at the house later?"

"Sounds like gossip time, and the husbands get roasted. No, I'm good. I've got a couple of friends I need to touch base with, then I'll be home."

She gave me a peck on the check, I suspect, to mark me as her territory. Callie nodded to both of us and walked away.

"What a beautiful wife," Sharon said. "Isn't it, or wouldn't it be wonderful, to have the kind of faith she seems to have? I really envy that."

"Yeah, we're the facts versus faith household. I think we're moving in the same direction, just from different angles."

"I'm a little confused. You're studying Jesus the man, but you are uncertain if he was Christ. So is this just a historical interest you have? Do you mind if I ask if you are religious?"

I stretched my legs, leaned back, but didn't look at her. "I'm a wannabe Christian. Actually I'm a wannabe believer that some god even exists. I'll take any god as long as he offers me an escape hatch out of here. Sounds totally selfish, but…"

"A fellow traveler," Sharon mused. "I've pretty much worked through the belief in the God of the Bible problem, which was a problem in my marriage with a good Jewish husband immersed in the Old Testament."

Her eyes lightened up as her erudition showed on her favorite subject. "My path to a fairly strong belief in God the creator, the unimaginable mind, came through my study of particle physics as it relates to the disbursement of matter and anti-matter. There could have easily been no universe with matter canceling itself out."

"What makes me think there is God is the old question of how could something come from nothing? What was before the big bang if not God?" I asked.

"That's part of my field of study. It's called the zero-point field or the quantum vacuum. In quantum mechanics that means there is no such thing as nothing, as you say. Electromagnetic waves and particles appear and disappear, even in what we think is nothingness."

"Whoa, whoa," I stopped her. "You've just sailed over the nothingness in my head."

She giggled. "Sorry, we live in a very strange universe of mysterious particles where nothing can be something. Where particles just appear. This whole discussion of whether there was nothing was started by Plato and Aristotle, who said there could be no vacuum. It wasn't until the 1600's that Blaise Pascal proved there could be a vacuum or nothing. Or so he thought.

"Isn't it interesting that in 2010 we are still debating over whether there was once nothing?" She shook her head at the oddity of the thought.

"What I would call craziness is what has brought you to God. God makes sense. Crazy doesn't," I concluded, feeling a comfort in her words and reasoning.

"Hey, I have an answer when someone asks me what brought me to God. I answer 'nothing.'" We both laughed.

"You're too smart for school," I offered lamely (one of my son's comments). "I remember the students like you when I was at Athens High. We called them The Brainiacs. And I secretly envied their easy intelligence."

"I may have been smart," she shook her head and her hair flowed away from her face in a subtle, sensual way. "But I was too tall and too thin, so I hid. Mathematics became my boyfriend and date." Her grin covered what obviously had been a long and hurtful part of her life.

"Well," I gave her an appraising look, "no point in hiding in the books anymore."

"I'll take that as a compliment and head back to Jesus."

"A very safe place to head to," I agreed.

"Through studying the exquisite impossibilities that had to occur for this universe to have been created, I have become a believer in the God of the Bible. It has been the result of statistical probabilities and logic," she said.

"Ah, so you did reason your way to heaven, to quote my wife. I'll admit I feel a sense of relief that someone may have found God through reasoning and not just accept it on faith." And I did have that sense of relief, though her discovery didn't mean I could reach the same conclusion. And she did finally have to have faith.

"I like to think that all physicists are spiritualists and romantics at heart. We marvel more than most at the excruciating fragility of the underlying ratios that had to be or we wouldn't exist. I feel my work has made me realize how the mind of God works. And it works mathematically." She gave a short laugh. "I get paid to study God the mathematician."

"I thought God's language was the language of love. Now we've got to add a new gospel about how to add and subtract if you want to really communicate with the Lord." I couldn't resist kidding.

I was more and more intrigued by this woman who was becoming too attractive and too attracting. And I felt I was sitting next to a fountain of knowledge that I thirsted for. "So why are you paying an archeologist to learn more about Jesus, who you don't think was God's son?"

"It's a part of this process of discovery I'm going through. The God of the Old Testament is too distant, too abstract, really, though I am convinced that a mind, a God, if you will, did create us. But I selfishly need a God I can get my arms around, a Jesus. I don't believe at this time that he was divine. But I'm still working on it."

She took a slow sip of wine then lowered it and looked at me. "Skepticism can be healthy. It drives you to investigate. You can be a thinker and a Christian at the same time. So where are you on the religion scale?" She asked the now familiar question I always tried to avoid.

"I was raised in the Methodist church. I'm about to be an elder in the Presbyterian Church. We've got to tell that glowing moment when Christ came into our lives. I wish I could say with conviction it had happened."

"And why do you wish you were, I assume, a Christian?" she asked.

I replied honestly, "Culture probably. I don't relate to Islam or Hinduism. If I had been raised around it, I would probably be wondering if Mohammed was for real. Let's be honest. Aren't most people trying to believe out of totally selfish reasons? I know I'm supposed to say my life goal is to serve the Lord if I'm going to be a Christian, but I'm concluding it's all about serving me and really serving my fears."

"Still you're searching," she correctly surmised.

"I've always loved science and read it on a number of subjects, and I realize my wanting to live is a basic impulse of life. All life is programmed to do what it takes to stay alive. The impulse to survive is an imperative for everything from grass to humans. We are wired to survive, not to die. But that didn't start out as my motivation for doing some research on Jesus."

I looked at both of our glasses. "This conversation is getting a little heavy. How about another glass of wine?"

"I need to study the physics of that; alcohol reduces heaviness." Her mouth pushed her right cheek out when she grinned. I was noticing too much about her. Too many of the features of her face, her nuances and mannerisms. As I took her glass, my fingers touched hers and I was aware of how a feather-light touch of skin has its own secret world of delight.

As I started for the bar, several people walked over to her and immediately engaged her in an animated conversation. She was one of Atlanta's heavy hitters who attracted the empty pocket charity board members to her deep pockets.

The line to the bar was thick with third and fourth timers, all robust in their laughter as they shouldered and shuffled along as though their ankles were tied.

When I returned to Sharon, she was surrounded by a small group of people, so I stood modestly to the side, not wanting to interrupt. But she interrupted their conversation by moving toward me and announcing, "Excuse me, please, I must show Mr. McGrath an architectural problem he might solve." And with that we headed toward a large hallway out of the main floor.

As we moved away from three hundred aggressively socializing patrons of the arts, the silence in the hallway was soothing. It opened into several gallery rooms. What in the world could I advise her on in this perfectly manicured place?

"I'm studying Jesus the man because of a harebrained idea I had while playing golf. Some friends and I are into or looking at retirement and wondered if Jesus had lived to 65 and then been killed, would his life have been a guide for retirees."

She stopped and grinning said, "Well, that's inventive. I like it. I don't think it's harebrained at all. So how are you going about finding your information?"

"Calling up professors, my minister, an archeologist; one person leads to the next. Believe me, Jesus as a man is a subject I know next to nothing about, but I've gotten caught up in it and am finding it fascinating."

She acknowledged that she understood my attraction to searching for the unusual. "The thrill of the chase. That's what I do for a living. I chase after the truth, I like to think. Discovery is exhilarating. By the way, who is the archeologist?"

We had stopped in front of a gallery filled with displays of Egyptian wall art and statues. "You would have loved this guy; very colorful, rambunctious I would say. Had a strange name, Judah Akhen."

Her face lit up in surprise and laughter. She grabbed me by my arm and exclaimed, "I can't believe it! I'm co-sponsoring Judah's dig. Is this too small a world or what?"

I probably looked as surprised as she did. "You're the one!" It suddenly came to me that she was the woman he wanted me to talk with. "Judah had given me a name for me to speak to, and I now remember it was you."

"Another little God thing. They just pop up all the time," she smiled.

"Judah told me about wanting to dig in Israel, but said he needed funding from National Geographic. Isn't he a hoot? Now that's a dig I would like to go on." Our common interest was drawing me more and more into her.

"Well, I'll be there for two weeks. And Judah is going to get a partial grant from the Geographic Society. I'm funding the rest. You should bring your wife and come on over."

I felt a tinge of guilt because I felt a tinge of disappointment that she had suggested I bring my wife. "That brings up an interest-

ing point of conflict between us. She resists trying to prove anything about Jesus, while I can't accept much of it on faith alone."

We stood at the entrance to the gallery, as though our conversation had its own constraints, which wouldn't allow us to be
distracted by the faded, but still fabulous colors of the hieroglyphics
in the room.

I felt I was getting into a personal area, discussing Callie, so
I quickly moved away. "Tell me, where is this dig exactly and what
do you think it could tell you about Jesus?"

"It's at the seaport that used to be Capernaum. I know Judah
feels Jesus ministered from there. He is digging in what were the
docks during Jesus' life. He's unearthing a house near where Peter
lived," she answered.

Shrugging her shoulders, she said with an expectant joy, "I
don't know what we might find, but my imagination has us digging
up an old wooden writing tablet with the wax still on it with one of
Jesus' sayings written in the wax as he was saying it. Totally won't
happen, but isn't pretending exhilarating and freeing?"

She was so refreshing and into the subject of my search that
I wasn't just taken with her exuberance for life and its mysteries,
I was also taken with her. While searching for the perfect man I
knew damn well that my imperfect thoughts were condemning me.
What a joke all of this is. What if I start to think Jesus is Christ?
What if I start believing, yet I'm still capable of being attracted to
a woman I met 30 minutes ago? What a hypocrite.

Looking into her face I said, "I never thought of science being
grounded not just in fact but also in fantasy. You sound like a child
on an Easter egg hunt, driven by the mystery of where the eggs may
lie and what their color may be."

"Oh, life should be a big Easter egg hunt everyday. What is
more fun than discovery! How many nights have I spent looking

up at the stars and imagining which ones I will find that have that distinct wobble when they have planets revolving around them, and which planets may have life forms."

"So what have you imagined about Jesus the man and what do you know? Have you really been studying up on him?" I asked her.

"I met Judah at a biblical archeological conference at the Carlos Museum at Emory. I had rounded the corner about believing in God but wanted a relationship and became intensely interested in Jesus. I love archeology and attended the conference just out of curiosity. There I met Judah and my journey of discovering about Jesus the man started."

She motioned with her head toward the gallery we stood before, and we stepped inside. Spreading her arm out in a sweeping motion, she said, "Jesus won't be found in here. As you can see, this is an Egyptian art collection that our family foundation has sponsored. The necklaces, bowls, wall paintings, all come from the time Moses left Egypt, around 1220 BC. That's why my foundation agreed to pay for its shipment and care. It's an intense experience that has drawn very large audiences in Atlanta."

"This is stunning." I said. The jewelry and art of that most glorious of all ancient civilizations stood like intensely colored exclamation marks against the stark white walls of the gallery. "I think it's a very intense experience to see life frozen like this."

I was suddenly concerned about how much time I had left with her, so I turned the subject back to Jesus. "Let's change the subject. How would you characterize Jesus as a man?"

"Well, if you read all that the four gospels reveal, he was one who appeared to have changed his life at middle age, about 35 years old. But I suspect he was always that confrontational, narrow-focused, unflinching, fiery personality. You just don't wake up one day from being your everyday mild-mannered carpenter to being

Mister Charismatic; a man ready to duke it out intellectually with the nearest Pharisee," she answered.

"So you think Jesus could have always been known by friends as a man who loved God fiercely. But apparently he wasn't promoting or marketing his message until he met John the Baptist."

"Possibly. I am constantly trying to mix rational thinking with the knowledge that there will always be a mystery with Jesus. Still, it is irrational to me for this man to be just another construction worker on the docks and then he's suddenly a religious trailblazer of unmatched brilliance in his oratorical skills. My imagining, my attempts to figure the man out, say he was an emerging spiritual leader."

"Emerging?" I queried. "He was born God, I thought."

"It's a term most Christians don't like or accept. Yes, to them he was God from the moment of his birth. Jesus was not born totally human and then transitioned into the divine. There was no transforming over the years into the Christ of the New Testament to those who knew him."

"No worm to butterfly kind of thing." It was my weak attempt to come up with a metaphor I could understand. "But in your emerging Christ I still don't see how any rational thinking allows a man to turn into a god."

"How does a worm turn into a butterfly?" She grinned in a kind of loopy way. "I shouldn't have used that because I know how that molecular process works. Maybe God changed the man into the Christ at the quantum particle level where all is uncertain." She shrugged, "This kind of speculation gets silly, doesn't it, and I can see why it annoys your wife. That's where mystery and faith come in."

We were slowly walking around the gallery room and were standing next to a long wall painting of Egyptians in a boat fishing. "My image of the man is that he was so passionate that he had little patience even for his disciples when they doubted or were confused about him. Jesus was a radical in confronting the religious hierarchy in Jerusalem. He was an amazing debater, speaker, and was very social. He loved the tradition of table and teaching while eating. He was a first class schmoozer, though that does sound disrespectful, doesn't it?" She looked at me almost apologetically.

"No, it sounds like you are trying to make the man current; bring him in to today's world so we can understand him. So he's not this abstract perfect person who few can relate to."

"It's a puzzling aspect of Jesus, that though his work put him at the bottom of the social ladder, he dined and debated regularly with priests, scribes, lawyers, and well-off tax collectors. This is puzzling because his lowly station should not have given him the credibility for someone of wealth and position to invite him into their home for a meal and give a hoot about what he said."

I mulled over her words. "Maybe his intellect was so obvious, so compelling, that he overcame being a lower class worker. Or what if he weren't a carpenter on a construction site after all? Maybe Jesus spent his twenties in thought on the nature of man and God. Maybe he was recognized as a forcefully articulate interpreter of a new slant on Judaism."

"Hmmm. True, in the Gospels he would go off alone for hours and restore his energies through prayer. Possibly he spent great periods in contemplation, in cleansing his own mind of the corrosive desires to seek wealth and power. He knew the desire to own was its own god. He was seeking a direct, unhindered line between a man's heart and the Lord."

We had remained alone in the room. I don't know how long we had talked, but the noise from the crowd in the main hall seemed to be softening. Perhaps the party was winding down. I had forgotten to ask her what she wanted me to advise her on as an architect, but now assumed it was just an excuse for us to get away from the crowd. With her deep pockets and contacts I assume she was constantly sought after, even hounded, by organizations needing money. Maybe our talking had been a refreshing escape from all the charity boards that took these galas as a chance to cozy up to her Big Bucks.

"I apologize for pulling you away from your friends, but I've never met someone so actively pursuing with their money the reality of Jesus from a analytical standpoint. I'll have to say I find you very interesting."

Her pale-colored lips opened in an easy, teasing smile. "First, I look like somebody from Aspen; now I'm very interesting. Your compliments themselves are interesting, Mr. McGrath. Or should I say juvenile and unpracticed."

"Very unpracticed. You got me. Been married too long. Lost my luster on flattering women. So before you leave me in a room filled with 3,000 year old artifacts, let me ask you what you think Jesus' life must have been like in his 60's?"

She walked over to a glass case with a display of little wooden figures, like toys, but very realistic, all portrayed on a fishing boat. A plaque read that the figures had been buried in a tomb around 2,000 BC.

Looking thoughtfully into the case, she said, "My guess would be that Jesus moved to one of the port towns on the Sea of Galilee at the north end of the sea, and was a fisherman and a teacher, but in a quieter manner. Antipas had already sent him back to Pilate, seeing no threat in his teaching. He may have stayed in Antipas' governing territory. So there was safety as long as he stayed quiet. But spies for Antipas were everywhere. They would tell the governor if Jesus started drawing big crowds again, which

were considered a threat by the Romans. The rebuttal to my scenario is it ignores the passion and fire that was a major part of Jesus'
personality."

"Let's see if I can complete your thought," I proposed. "I'm
trying to grasp some of this on my own. Jesus would have lived as
a resident teacher, working from his home in an unobtrusive manner with a small but dedicated following. And to support himself
he may have worked on Peter's boat. The only waves he would have
made would be in a boat, and not stirring up the masses."

I felt I was coming to an understanding the more I heard and
thought about the subject. "I'm thinking Jews and Gentiles would
come to listen to his teachings, debate with him alone or in small
groups. Some may have left as disciples. He would enjoy all of the
love and devotion of an honored, older wise man and prophet."

Sharon interjected, "I will tell you that this settled teaching and work life would have been easier had he married and had
a companion who helped with gardening and cooking. Obviously,
having children to work vineyards or barley fields in order to barter
for supplies would have made this existence easier as well as self-
sustaining. But having said this, the gospel narratives showed a man
very aggressive in 'selling his message', and it is unlikely he would
have relegated his often fiery personality to the quiet of some som-
nolent village, teaching the occasional pilgrim. But if he wanted
to live to be 65, he would have had to have backed off challenging
Jewish leaders out in public." She paused and a smile crept over her
face. "It would have been funny if Herod's son Antipas would have
asked Jesus to come and tell him more of his teachings. Actually,
that could have happened. Leaders were fascinated by prophets.
Maybe he felt guilty about having John the Baptist killed."

She twirled the empty wine glass stem between her fingers.
"Jesus was very social, as I said. But without a wife to cook, he

couldn't have had people for dinner. He could have been continually invited to the home of others. If he never married by age thirty-five when he was arrested, I doubt he ever married. It was a teenage thing in that day."

A security guard appeared at the door. "Excuse me, Mrs. Gold, but we have about ten minutes before the party ends."

Winding down our conversation, I then said, "I'll take these thoughts and compile them at some point on how I might turn this into retirement advice. I can't thank you enough for your generosity." I felt I was staring too intently at this dressed-in-beige creature.

We went back down the hall into the main floor where the party had thinned and those left were starting a slow move toward the door.

I didn't want the party, this party, to end. Impulsively I said, "Wish I could go to the digs. I'll bet there will be a papyrus rolled up in a jar with a detailed description on what Jesus looked like. And you'll find it."

"Your imagination is alive as it must be if you are to find the man," Sharon responded. "Bring your wife, or come yourself. We can always use people who are good with trowels. Got to run. Be in touch if you need to talk. So nice to have met you."

She stopped herself suddenly, put a hand on my arm and said, "Sonny, there is a freedom in believing that there is a real God. And it is not all faith. There is rationale that suggests very strongly that it's true. I hope you can find that truth."

She squeezed my arm, looked into my eyes for a second as though she were giving me a message. And it is in those moments that worlds turn and eternity dwells; when all of life is caught in a glorious touch, a mesmerizing glance which shines a brief light on an intense love that could be, but only in dreams. She then walked across the room to two friends who must have been her ride home.

Life is like a series of sentences. The moments can end as they normally do with a period. Others end in question marks, others in exclamation marks. And these sentences are singularities such as an event or a person that are so directional that life's course is reset and a new chapter started. But there could be no new chapter started here. Still, I felt I was following her walking away with a little too much longing as I headed for the door and my wife.

Callie was in the bathroom getting ready for bed when I got home. I went to the room I use as an unofficial office. I was checking my emails before going to bed and was pleased, too pleased, to see one had already come in from Sharon. I hesitated to click it open, enjoying the anticipation of what she might be writing to me about so quickly. I imagined it was some expression, some nuanced between-the-lines expression of how much she enjoyed our talk; even inviting me again to meet her at the dig in Israel.

I sat, hand hesitating on the mouse, seeing us, Sharon and me, not Callie and me, wearing flowing Lawrence of Arabia white robes at sunset in the columned ruins of a just-discovered temple, wine glasses in hand. My arm slides around her waist. The soft orange light paints us in ancient amber, and then she turns toward me as gently as the desert breeze lifting her hair and murmurs...

"Sonny. It's late. Let's go to bed," Callie ordered from the doorway to my home office. "What are you looking at this late?"

"Nothing, honey, just catching up on any late messages." And I clicked the mouse and closed the emails, not daring to open the anticipated one with my trusting and loving and Christian wife standing at my shoulder.

"Seemed like you and Sharon had a lot to talk about." Callie was probing and I knew it. She took her rings and bracelet off then slipped under the bed covers.

"We did," I answered, not trying to show too much enthusiasm. "It was weird, but that archeologist I talked to recently had recommended I meet her. Seemed ordained."

"She's a real player in the donor community. I always admired how carefully she uses her foundation's money. Hope she brought you closer to the Lord. Good night, sweetie."

As I lay next to this wonder woman, I allowed no more amber-colored robes, no delicate breezes, no more sunsets over the Sea of Galilee to paint my heart blacker than it normally was. It had been a distant dream.

Redemption eluded me as I was up early the next morning to check her email. It was not an invitation to a Mediterranean sunset, but a terse delivery of a name to call, with a hint of an invitation. It read: "Contact Hamilton Simpson: ham_simp825@gmail.com. I've already emailed him about your study. Think about the dig. We can always use a few new hands. Sharon."

I was sixteen again. Stupidly enthralled over a path I could never take. But guilty in the heart is guilty. I was filled with too much of a rush to deny that in a heartbeat I would be on a plane to see her, if I had that choice. I emailed Hamilton and asked if I could drop by his offices in pursuit of my study, saying Sharon had given me his name. He quickly replied with a 'Sure,' and a date to meet. I was a fallen soul, and I didn't give a damn. What religion would have me? And how could I do anything but lie to Jack?

Act Like Jesus

Jack's family had created one of those online caregiver sites from which you can receive daily reports on the condition of a sick friend or relative; an easy way for updates to be received without constantly calling the family. It's also a way to coordinate taking meals over. The word on Jack was that his melanoma had found a network of highways from his lymph nodes out to the key regions of his body and with dispatch the angry cells had established a beach-head in his lungs and probably outposts in his brain.

On Wednesday, August 22, Callie and I called Betty and asked if we could prepare a supper and bring it over Friday night. I was cooking salmon on the grill. Betty said that would be thought-ful, her voice heavy with both weariness and defeat, but still uplift-ing with gratitude.

Jack was depressed and very angry. What had it all been about, he constantly asked her. He didn't want to die. He had said several times that I was doing some important research for him. I was his messenger. Betty had an urgency about her voice when she talked to us, asking if I were searching for some miracle medicine.

I had to laugh after the call. Miracle medicine is exactly what I've been trying to discover. Callie didn't think it funny. She felt very saddened that Jack had never known Christ, and continued to think it utter nonsense that I was still 'thrashing around', as she called it, looking for Christ in all the wrong places. She would pray for grace to save him at the end.

Betty said, "We've had so many friends bring food, but they usually just leave it. Jack's too weak for any kind of a party, but he said he wants to have a light supper with some close friends while his mind is clear. So, Sonny, maybe see if Max and Phil want to drop by and possibly two of his closest law partners; so eight of us. It could be a nice celebration of Jack's life while he's still living."

Betty seemed pleased and we hung up.

The next day, Thursday, I called two of his close friends at his former law firm, partners who had profited by Jack's profligate rainmaking for years. All had plans for Friday night. Concert tickets for one and a weekend at The Cloisters for another partner; these trumped saying goodbye to the once mighty Jack Martin.

"Hey, Phil, Betty wants us to come over Friday for a drink with Jack." I reported over the phone.

There was a long pause, and Phil said softly, "Can't do it."

I was stunned. Phil had known Jack forever. "What do you mean?" I asked.

"I'll be honest with you, Sonny. Jack's dying has messed my head up in some strange ways. I've gotten really down about it, and coming to see him dying is a car wreck I just can't slow down for. I'll give him a call. I can do that, and I want to do that."

"I won't tell him I asked you. If he asks where you are, I'll say what, that you've got the flu? I don't know."

Phil's voice was as quiet as I had ever heard him. "No, I'll call tomorrow and we'll have some laughs, and I'll say I love him, and for that reason, if that makes sense, I want to say goodbye over the phone."

Phil, the man who always laughed at death, feeling comfort in his belief that it was a natural part of a world without purpose, suddenly couldn't face an ending that touched him.

I called Max. "Maxie, we're going over to Phil's for a quick supper Friday night. You're invited."

A long pause. "Can't. Wish I could. But I'm hosting some Muslims for a dinner. We're going to try and convert them. I visited with Jack a few days ago. Looked awful. I prayed with my hands on him. I prayed mightily, Sonny, but Jack is slipping away from us, and we have to let go and move to souls that we think we can save. Like these Muslims."

I was knocked speechless. Jack had been a golfing buddy of Max's for years. And yet he would rather convert Muslims he never met instead of making a last desperate attempt to save the soul of a friend? I was so mad and disappointed in Max, I clicked the phone off. I was resigned to Callie and me going, and that would just mean more quality time, a good thing.

The next morning I stopped at the Whole Foods on West Paces Ferry Road to pick up the salmon. To call it a grocery store is to defame it. This is a fantasy example of food in an acute state of its ultimateness. It's like a movie where the actors and scenery have been digitized into their most intense colors. And the prices reflect the high cost of glamour eating.

I parked and started to walk in when I heard a strangely familiar voice coming from behind. "Can you help a person out?" I didn't have to turn to know who it was. I stopped, shook my hand, and muttered, "I don't believe it."

It was she again, the homeless woman and her male friend. He was standing back a few steps, staring at the ground; his baseball cap pulled low, shadowing his reluctance, shame, whatever caused him in his own mind to hide in plain sight.

I said matter-of-factly, "Well, you two really cover a lot of ground. That's a long walk from Emory to Buckhead."

She stood an arm's length from me. She smelled very bad. She looked worse than before. Her hair put to music would have been an orchestra of drunks. Her teeth were even more yellowed with a piece of food stuck to one of them. Worse, she needed to blow her nose. *A little test from the Lord*, I thought to myself. *Or is the Lord in disguise?*

"Took us two weeks to get over here," she replied with some pride, "but we made it." By car Emory University is about twenty minutes away.

"Oh, it's you," she recognized me and seemed stunned and started to turn away. "It's him. Let's move on," she said to the man with her.

Why would they remember me from a month ago? Am I the only person who has turned them down? Then the words came out of my mouth with no force or premeditation by me.

"No, wait. How would you like to have supper with my wife and me?" *Who the hell asked that?*

She seemed frozen, then asked, "What do you mean?"

"Supper. Tomorrow night at a friend's house with my wife and me."

She stuttered in confusion, "I, I, don't understand." She was looking back and forth at me and then the man, who also had a quizzical look on his face.

"I'm serious. I'm offering you a nice supper with some good people. I can pick you up wherever you're living and take you back afterwards."

"Jose?" She asked for an answer in Spanish from her friend, who had timidly stood by until now. He raised his head for the first time in our two meetings, puffed his lips out in agreement, nodded, and said, "Si."

Her whole demeanor changed. She brushed her hand against her hair like she was trying to straighten it. Her eyes widened from their bleary look. "Okay. Yes. We will." Her voice flowed with a growing cheer.

Then, in a sudden realization, her voice sounded urgent and panicky. "I don't have clothes for this. Our clothes were stolen."

"Who cares? You look fine like you are." Had I lost my mind? Her clothing looked awful. Maybe Callie and Betty could give her some of their old clothes. Thinking of Callie for the first time, I realized I should have called and asked about this. But, no, she told me about the man who gave a feast and invited people he didn't know, which we had never done. This seemed like a move in the right direction for me, as admittedly out of left field as it was.

It was set. I would pick them up outside The Waffle House on Pharr Road. She said her name was Jenny and was from Alabama. The man with her was from Mexico, she said, and I assumed was here illegally. This was a test for me in this search for where I stood on tolerance, forgiveness, trying to see if I could live some of the scriptures. For Jack's sake and my story back to him, I was trying to immerse my mind in what I thought to be the mind of Jesus. The mind of meaning. He would have invited these outcasts in. Probably even washed their feet, but heaven will not see my sweet face if I've got to do that. No feet washing, Lord. Give me another assignment, please. I went home with the groceries and my secret guest list, thinking I would just walk into the dinner with them unannounced. I get stupid sometimes. I'm too impulsive, but sometimes jumping on an opportunity can open doors that otherwise would never open. If I were to find life's meaning through Christianity, I had to get my mind into it. To me, one way to start the process was to 'act like Jesus'. In that brief moment, this invitation to supper seemed like a good way to do that.

Who Do I Think I Am?

Historically, Atlanta's deep pockets have made their money as lawyers, accountants, in real estate, insurance and banking. I had a date with one of the movers at 7:30 Friday morning.

I had read about 'Ham' Simpson in a recent profile in The *Atlanta Business Chronicle*. He headed a large insurance company in Atlanta and led an investment group to buy several small struggling banks. His was a rare story of business success in an otherwise flat Atlanta market.

The article also called him a renaissance man, being a self-taught scholar and speaker on Roman history, a Himalayan mountaineer, and the organizer of a large men's Bible study group that many of the power players attended.

As I sat in his glass and steel reception room, I stared at the golf trophies he had won in various local tournaments. *What doesn't this man do?* I asked myself. Some people can make you feel like an absolute failure in life.

"Hey, Sonny. Good to meet you, buddy." He appeared like a burst of energy that just materialized. He seemed genuinely happy to meet me; a joy, I'm sure, everyone who met him felt.

Ham was about six feet, and thin. He was bald in the center of his head. His hair to the sides was brown with no gray, though he had to be over 55. His tanned and nicely creased face captured his outdoor play and adventures. His short nose was an afterthought. His whole being enjoyed his laugh, which, I would learn, accompanied many of his words.

"Well, it's not everyday I meet a bone fide renaissance man," I needled him.

"Those lying newspapers," he countered. "You know how you can't believe what you read anymore. Here, let's step in the conference room. We've got an executive board meeting in a little bit, so let's see if we can visit before the clamoring herd comes in."

We entered a long conference room with one wall all glass, giving a glamour shot view of downtown Atlanta. It was mesmerizing.

Knowing his schedule was tight, I said, "I recently met Sharon at The High, and she said I should grab a minute of your time about this unusual study I'm doing."

"Anyone Sharon Gold says you should meet, you meet. She's an amazing asset to this city. So how can I help you?"

We were sitting at one end of a long mahogany conference table in deep leather chairs. He sat close to me and leaned forward. I told him of how my search for Jesus as a guide for retirees had started, but now was a larger, more insane search for any meaning to this life. I said my dying friend was desperate to know if there was any hope for an afterlife. I then said I didn't know why Sharon thought he might help.

He whistled through his teeth and shook his head. "Now that's a big assignment, my friend. Sharon knows of my Bible study group, which was the result of a search I did years ago for life's meaning. I know that sounds a little heavy," he sounded apologetic, "but when I hit 50, I went through a depression about what the devil life was all about. I always thought it was pretty much about achievement. One of my closest friends actually died in my arms of a heart attack at the golf course at Capital City. It shook me deeply."

"I've not had any close friends die yet. They may be too pickled in alcohol. It has become their preservative," I joked.

We laughed. "Sounds like my crowd," he said. "Anyway, I decided to do a search, like you, except I went on a spiritual journey that included an intense study of the world's major religions. I talked to a lot of philosophers, mystics, atheists, theologians, all sorts of people."

"That's really fascinating," I responded with interest. "Did you just take off for a month or something?"

"I did." I told my wife and my partners that I'd never been so unhappy in my life, and I knew it sounded like a crazy midlife crisis thing, but I was going on a search for whatever I was looking for."

"I'll bet your wife said the truth was that you had lost your mind, right?"

"You've got it!" he congratulated me in his enthusiastic way. "But I felt so damn lost. I had to get away, and I did for almost two months. I went to Tibet and fasted for days on a mountainside. I met with mystics in Ethiopia. I went to a Sioux Indian sweat tent and then a sun dance ceremony where I had a sharpened bone stuck through the skin on my chest with a rope attached to it that's pulled tight. The skin stretched and ripped until I fainted. Later, I spent a week with a New Age guru in California."

"Good Lord. I feel my little study is pretty pathetic." I did feel diminished.

"Interesting that you said, 'Good Lord', because that was the end result of my search for meaning. And I started out as an agnostic. No, probably an atheist."

A young man with short, spiked hair and an untucked blue shirt came quietly into the room and began setting up a lap top and projector at the other end of the table.

Ham ignored him. I said, "So you found religion, as they say."

He sat back in the cushioning of the chair. "My wife's exact words when I finally returned. She said you didn't need to be gone for two months. You could have found that at Peachtree Road Methodist in Buckhead." A loud, short laugh ushered out at this statement.

"No, I didn't find religion, but I found purpose and belief I had never had. I found what Leo Tolstoy concluded, that love is the driving force, the basis for meaning in this life. And this love described the business model, if you will, for a God who cares."

"So you took all that you had heard across the globe and your conclusion is that there is God, number one, and number two, this God is active in our individual lives. This was no clockmaker who just set it running and passively watches it tick," I concluded.

"You got it. But let's get away from me. As you can see, we're setting up for a meeting in a bit. Let me tell you an angle I have as a businessman on Jesus the man."

Before he could start, I curiously added, "I didn't know you had studied Jesus as a man."

"Oh yes. Since I started a Bible study, I felt I needed to make Jesus relatable to a number of the men that I knew were basically coming to network. I knew they were cafeteria Christians, if you will; a little Jesus here, a little there, but they never went for the entree."

"So to reel in the reluctant fish, you baited them with Jesus the businessman," I surmised.

"Correct. Here are some of my thoughts that might be of help to you. In business terms, Jesus left the world of being an employee of building contractors to become an entrepreneur, starting his own 'company'. The business model of this new company was to create a life-changing communication service that was operated by twelve very loyal employees, the disciples. None would be paid, so the CEO, Jesus, had to be a top-flight motivator. His mission, his branding and positioning, were crystal clear and accepted eventually with enthusiasm by the employees."

"This was a nonprofit company. So where did the financing come from?" I asked.

"Angel investors, no pun intended. Patrons, I believe, who were widowed women mostly, who gave the company a little money to eat on, but mostly gave food outright. Since they walked everywhere and slept on the rooftops of supporters, they just needed help with food."

I interjected, "The corporate goal was to create a strong support system that would spread the company's message around the Mediterranean area."

"Yep. Jesus was both product and messenger. His message was that the old Jewish model built around observance of the laws and the hierarchy of the temple priests needed challenging. But his new idea built around rejecting the approach of the existing model had him at a handicap from the start. His business model demanded he be confrontational with the old guard, abrupt, unyielding, and also very demanding of both his twelve employees and his clients or converts. This may have seemed like a paradox because the positioning and his message were built around love, grace, and forgiveness. The whole operation had a feminine feel to it for its day, which made it a truly unique product."

"I would say he was an unparalleled motivator, whose charisma and message could get working men to leave their jobs and come and work for no pay," I added.

"The essential element in the Jesus business plan was that the founder was going to leave the company. He was going to allow himself to be killed. This meant that ultimate success demanded that his message go viral. The business depended on committed employees, if you want to call the disciples that," Ham said.

"In marketing parlance he had to create buzz," I observed.

"And he did with miracles," Ham agreed.

"In the end, it was a business model that appeared to have failed; he had let everyone down. His brand was abandoned by all the company's employees, because he had positioned himself as either God's son, or one who had a very close relationship with God, and there he lay beaten to a pulp and dead," Ham said.

I was seeing the whole scene in Jerusalem with a greater clarity. "And as he had stood before Pilate, he seemed powerless to his disciples and converts. Certainly no Messiah."

"Yeah. But he had a spectacular way of closing the sale." Ham gave me a great set up.

"Nothing like rising from the dead." I guess I'll never lose my cynicism.

We both laughed. Ham said, "I know all of this sounds silly, this talk of his running a business, but I swear this kind of story illustrates the lengths I have to go to get some men to start a relationship with Jesus. I have to put it in business terms. But then Jesus spoke to the tone of his times, so why don't I?"

Ham continued, "In that line of thinking, Jesus knew how to run a business. His first move was to bring on employees, or disciples. They were expected to learn his message in depth, which allowed them to go in advance of him into villages to draw crowds and perhaps make sure there was food to be donated."

I was catching on quickly to this business analogy. "So Jesus' methodology of setting up his ministry insisted that the business be driven in part by equally aggressive, product-smart, brand-aware, self-starting disciples. But would they as a group, each of whom had families to feed, be willing to follow him in extended missionary trips out of Galilee into other lands?"

Ham frowned, "Not so fast on giving the disciples too much initial credit. Jesus saw his positioning had not made his twelve as savvy about just what his message was. That uncertainty caused him to ask them, 'Who do you think I am?'"

"What did those who knew Jesus think of him?" I asked.

"Before his ministry started, by the reactions of people who knew him, Jesus appears to have led a normal artisan's life; certainly nothing that foretold he would become a brilliant debater; a charismatic parable-speaking, revolutionary messenger."

"I do remember when he spoke in Nazareth his own townspeople tried to kill him. What's that about?" I asked.

I was realizing that to me the Jesus story is a strange encounter for those who try and understand its duality. The perfect man, miracle worker, God's son on the one hand, but a man who bled and cried out in anguish from the cross on the other hand.

"Yes, that's Mark 6. Jesus is teaching in his hometown and the reaction is one of shock. They asked, 'Where did this man get this idea that the Old Testament is fulfilled in him? What rabbi taught him? Isn't this the carpenter? Isn't this Mary's son?' That passage closes by saying that Jesus was amazed at their lack of faith."

Whether true or not, I believed I was starting to fill in the blanks I had on the Jesus story. "The rejection by people who had known him all his life says they didn't think he was special at all. This passage would say Jesus had said no memorable parables, given no unique interpretations, and performed no miracles for his entire life up to that point when he was about 35. To his hometown he was just another carpenter guy."

"Don't over read that event. They may have known him as a holy man, but not a revolutionist. But again, possibly the event was revealing of what Jesus was, or rather wasn't doing, in his 20's," Ham added.

"Well, he surely wasn't out being the Jesus we know." I had never thought much about Jesus in his 20's before.

Ham said, "You know I kind of like this Jesus from a human standpoint. He made a spectacular break from his life in middle age, and 35 was definitely middle-aged back then."

I nodded. "Talk about one of the all time great rebranding jobs. From nobody carpenter that his own townspeople wanted to kill, to world changer who had people willing to die for him."

"On the face of it, Jesus seems to have led two totally different lives, but I suspect that his twenties were a time of intense spiritual development. His appearance at the Jordan was not a sudden emergence."

The young man at the end of the table was setting up a teleconference with a client in England. A picture appeared on a wall screen, showing another conference room with people gathering in it. The young assistant then looked at Ham and said, "Ham, we've got about ten minutes."

I felt the urgency of needing to get to my main question. "If you can imagine Pilate releasing Jesus and his not being crucified until in his 60's, what do you think he would have been doing?" I asked quickly.

"Sonny, let's step out here. We're going to have eight noisy associates arriving any minute."

We talked while we stood near the glass door entrance into the lobby. "Death was a common act back then," Ham continued. "Child birth was a death-defying act. Diarrhea from bad water was a constant killer. Infections from cuts, malnutrition, you name it and dying was easy. But people did live long lives and Jesus, who may have been hardy physically, could have made it to his 60's. Oh, as a footnote, I believe his ministry was one year at the most."

"You think it was that short?" I asked.

"I do. Many believe it was three years. I don't see how he would have been allowed by the Jewish leaders or Pilate to draw crowds for that long. It would also have been difficult to support the disciples and the growing followers with food and lodging for three years. The disciples were working men. They had families to feed. But obviously, their faith in him, at least for a period of time, overrode all of these concerns."

I suggested, "Maybe the movement would have slowed appreciably after Pilate beat him unmercifully and then let him go. He would have been seen as toxic by the disciples now that Pilate knew of him."

"Right. If his ministry had faltered, since the end of days did not come nor did he appear to be the Messiah, he may have had no choice but to return to construction or fishing work. He would have remained committed to his immense love of God, but would be known around construction sites as a Godly brick layer who performed an occasional healing."

I was getting a feel for the exquisite timing of Jesus' crucifixion happening when it did. I suggested to Ham, "Yes, but from all I am hearing about Jesus, with the burning intensity he was exhibiting in the Gospels, it seems unlikely that he would abandon his midlife change and return to laying bricks and stone for the homes of the wealthy. He likely would have continued his mission, but on a far smaller scale. He would have been dependent on family or a few patrons for support, perhaps by women whom he championed. He would not have been known as Christ until he was crucified later."

From where we stood we could see staff members heading for the conference room.

Ham saw them too and seemed to want to get more thoughts out before we parted. "To have survived that long, I see Jesus in self-imposed exile just over the border in what is now Egypt, Syria or Lebanon. He would have had to work to eat, but was absorbed in both prayer and teaching to those who came to him. A really intriguing sidebar would have been Paul, who at some point may have come after Jesus. Paul could have been a lifelong adversary, or upon meeting Jesus, had the same blinding conversion and been Jesus' main disciple until his death."

"That would have been the A Team, the Dream Team wouldn't it? Jesus and Paul traveling and converting. I like that. Or Paul, who was so damn aggressive in whatever he pursued, could have seen in Jesus an exciting candidate to be a fellow Pharisee and tried to recruit him for that priesthood." My imagination was now off the charts with wild speculation.

"So Jesus retooled his business model down a little in order to keep the business going for thirty more years. Refreshed, reinvigorated, he returned to Palestine, drew thousands again, and a new ruler would have condemned him to death. And Christ would have emerged again." Ham concluded.

I knew it was past my time to go. "I can't thank you enough. I may have to check out your Bible study group. But it sounds like you all are a lot further along than I am."

Ham grinned broadly and put his arm on my shoulder. "Listen. Not only can you come anytime, but I may also have you as a guest speaker. You are on a journey to find where your mind should live, or a pilgrimage to discover a truth your core desperately yearns for. Many, many men are struggling just like you with their faith or lack of it. I would leave you with this conclusion: you have spent your life trying not to embrace him, and it has left you unfulfilled. Why not try for a while to accept him as truth? Throw away all the rational reasons you don't believe. Just try it. This embrace may just make you a new man."

I nodded in reluctant agreement. "Maybe."

"No maybe. Maybe doesn't work in life." He pointed his finger at me in a half serious way. "Open your heart to his love just once. It's quite a feeling," he said softly.

I cocked my head to one side and looked down in contemplation. "Jesus asked, 'Who do you think I am?' Maybe I should be asking who do I think I am?"

Ham nodded. "That may be the most profound question we can ask ourselves. The answer will be the guidepost for the rest of your life. You are definitely on a worthy search that too few people make. So stick with it."

I thought for a moment and concluded, "I think I've gotten lost in the Jesus at 65 pursuit. I see now it was just a ruse to get me thinking about life's meanings and God or no God. But it has moved me into places I've never gone in my mind; so, a good thing."

We both turned and I left filled with Ham's words. The waters of this voyage had gotten awfully deep.

Of All the Idiotic Things

Had my rush for meaning become a series of impulsive acts, jerking here, reaching there, like a falling man grasping for a branch? As suddenly as I had invited the homeless couple to come and eat with us, by Friday morning I began thinking I was crazy. Jack was dying. This was to be a loving goodbye among close friends, not among the kind of people he would never have associated with other than a rare dollar handout from his car. So some better judgment brain cell stepped up and said, *Bad idea.* The tough part was how could I tell the woman she couldn't eat with us. I thought I would run it by Callie, telling her the whole idea had just been that, an idea, and I wasn't going through with it. With the homeless woman expecting to come, maybe Callie would know what to say.

Callie saw my name on her cell phone and answered, her voice was somber. "Hey. My heart has really been on Jack and our getting with him tonight. I want us to put our hands on him together and for you to lead a prayer. If there has ever been a time for God in your life, it's now."

"Well, my laying hands on a dying man would be about as novel an idea as the one I've already had," I said. "I think you will be surprised. In a good way." I was feeling a little cheery about my idea.

Her voice was welcoming to my comment. "Surprised?"

"Luke gave me the idea," I teased.

There was a pause. "Luke? Luke who? What idea?"

"You know I told you about running into a homeless couple out at Emory, and that I gave them my usual crude and rude rejection. Well, these same two people came up to me yesterday at Whole Foods. They had migrated to Buckhead."

"I hope you were nicer to them this time," she scolded in her gentle way.

"Oh, I was a lot nicer. I invited them to eat with us tonight at Jack's. I got the idea from that verse you like so much in the book of Luke." My voice was filled with anticipation for her reaction.

"You did what!" She yelled. "Are you out of your mind? You can't do that!"

I pulled the phone away from my ear, unprepared for this explosion.

"Callie, I thought you would think it was a great idea. That's one of your favorite verses."

She fumed, "This is a private dinner for a man that's dying. It's not open to the public. That's an imposition on Betty and certainly on Jack. Of all the idiotic things you've done, this tops them all."

Callie has a natural, even voice, southern, but not a drawl. But these words were hammers, spears; sharp and heavy objects rendering my sensibilities into a state of confusion, defensiveness and then anger.

"Wait a minute, Callie. You're all the time on my case for not being a Christian, then I try and do a Christian act and I get blasted."

Her voice lowered and became more steely and probing. "Okay, Sonny, what's the real reason for this? Is this another story you can laugh at with the boys on the golf course? Another locker room tale, I suspect. Or was it to try and set me up with a test of my faith?"

It hurt that she thought I would do something like this just to laugh about. We may be cynics in the grill, but not like this. "I was just moved to do it. I had no thoughts of anything. I didn't even feel it was me asking them."

"Well, you're not doing it. This is beyond insulting to two of our best friends." Her voice rose again, "And to a dying friend. It's like a tasteless, practical joke."

I paused, then said calmly, "Don't worry. I've already backed off the idea. But you might tell me how I tell a homeless woman who's excited about a good meal, that she's now being canned."

"That," she said emphatically, "is your problem." She paused, still unable to comprehend why I had done this. "Why, Sonny? Were you trying to get a laugh out of Jack by laughing at these people?"

"Give me credit. My sense of humor doesn't sink to that level. Okay, two reasons. Jack's best friends all had excuses for not coming; weak excuses. Maybe this little study I'm doing has gotten into my head. So I reached out to the kind of people we would never invite to dinner, just like the rich man in the parable. I saw it as an act of kindness. Secondly, I wanted to show Jack that this is the kind of act that a Christian would do. If Jack wants to go to the heaven we imagine, then he would have to accept this homeless person in his home. He wants a message; this would be a message."

"No, this would be nonsense. Is Jack supposed to see some bedraggled woman standing next to him and have a last minute conversion? Is there a better word than *stupid*? No, you thought it would be funny. Even in your best friend's death, you've got to be a school boy, saying 'look at me.'"

I sat for a minute, thinking through this debacle. I have in 24 years of marriage only known Callie to get this mad maybe two times. It shook me up for the strange, alien tenor of her voice; a level of anger that was not her. A shrieking depth of anger that I didn't know she was capable of. And for her disavowing, almost violently, any trust that I could have an idea that could remotely approach Christian love…this hurt. Had it brought out a basic level of distrust and disrespect she always had for me and for my ability to do anything selfless and kind?

My mind roiled with emotions; mad at her, mad at me, doubting my ability to do anything right as far as Christian living goes, but especially fed up with my trying to bring a message about life's meaning to Jack.

When I extended the invitation, I had no idea why I went so out of character. But the more I thought about it, the more I liked it. I was sticking my toe in the waters of trying to see if there is a force called 'love' that gives meaning to this life, whether that meaning is Jesus or Mohammed. I was searching for meaning through acting out, not just thinking about it. I was trying, in what I thought a baby step, to get into this love and caring force embodied in Christianity and think in my way how Jesus would have reacted to Jenny. I was trying to be like him for the first time in my life. And it backfired big time.

On Friday evening we drove down through the tree garden called West Paces Ferry Road. Shadowed by hardwoods that enfold the street in a protective canopy, it is Buckhead's major east-west thoroughfare for seeing The Big Houses that the area has become world famous for.

Callie had said little. She was remote, disappointed, not to mention mad as hell. I was in full retreat on the idea, but it was too late. I had to tell this woman there would be no supper tonight.

We pulled into the Waffle House parking lot on Pharr Road.

She was standing outside, arms folded, no hat on, and her hair had some semblance of an attempted combing.

"There she is," I said. "Any ideas?" I gave a belated request to Callie as I parked a few feet away from the woman. No words had a chance of emerging from the tightness of Callie's lips.

I got out and walked over to her. "Hey, Jenny. Good to see you. Ready for some good food?"

She appeared a little shy, but nodded and said, "I've been looking forward to it all day. Even got my hair combed."

"Where's Jose? Inside?"

She seemed matter of fact. "He was picked up right after we saw you by the immigration people."

"Sorry about that, but look, I've got some bad news and some good news." I was trying to be firm and upbeat. My voice masked how badly I was feeling.

"I wanted you to come to a dinner at the home of a friend, but he is too sick to see more than a few people at a time. He has cancer and tonight isn't feeling well."

"Cancer? What was I ever going there for anyway? Were you going to show him a human that was in worse shape than he was? That was not fair to either one of us." Her indignation rose as she talked until she had a fierce look.

"Not fair," She yelled in a near-hysterical tone.

She looked around me at Callie sitting a few feet away in the car and spoke forcefully and with a noticeable anger. "And what does the lady in the car say? Do you know you're riding with a liar?"

I thought she had lost her mind, but in a calm voice from the dark of the car, Callie concurred. "It's true, his friend is very sick. We hope you understand."

"Oh, I understand. I remember Mister Not Fair from Emory. He was Mister Mean then. Now in Buckhead he's Sorry Liar!"

I felt this had entered the Theatre of the Absurd, and I tried to gain some control. People in the Waffle House were looking out the window at her obvious anger. I wondered who would call the police first.

"Here's the good news. I'm buying you supper anyway. I promised that you would get something to eat tonight, and I want to make sure you do. Here you go." I handed her two fifty-dollar bills I had folded in my pocket.

"Let me give you a ride to the shelter you're staying in and you can eat near there."

"My shelter is right here. Don't need a ride."

I was puzzled. "There's no shelter here. We're in the middle of Buckhead."

She managed a short laugh. "That's right, Mister. No rest for the weary in the land of the big houses. Ship 'em out of our precious Buckhead. Herd 'em downtown." She looked across the street at a dark ravine of brush and trees that had once been a streambed.

"When I visit Buckhead, my shelter's over there," she said.

"You might say I have a leaf mattress. But it's safe."

She then looked at the denomination of the bills and jolted me with her sarcasm as she held the bills up. "Well, buy me off. You must have a lot of guilt about this, Mister Liar. And now you're feeling good about yourself, aren't you? Bought the dirty hag off. Well, I'm taking it. Going to eat the Waffle House out of food, then finding me a Motel Six and going to sleep like rich folks tonight."

She tipped the two bills against her forehead in a salute, stepped to the restaurant door, turned and yelled, "Liar!"

Callie, gracious to the end, had gotten out, walked up to the retreating lady and stuck her hand out. Her fine features caught the earthy afternoon sun colors as it was setting. Her long nose and broad lips were accentuated in a honey-layered beauty.

"I'm Callie. I'm sorry this happened to you. But I'm the one who told Sonny that this was a bad idea. His friend is dying and

you're right, it wouldn't have been fair to you or Jack, his friend."
She lingered through a moment where they both seemed frozen, as
both tried to find clarity. Callie concluded, "Let's be truthful; he
had a stupid idea."

Callie's approach was so woman-to-woman and respectful
and honest that Jenny's posture became more erect, her face suddenly pleasant, even confident.

"I wish you the best and pray God will bless and protect you,"
Callie said with an assuredness that she felt God was there and
watching over this testimonial to a hard life.

Jenny smiled for the first time. "I feel He already has." And
she walked into the restaurant and out of our lives.

The car roared with silence when we both got back in. We
watched for a moment as Jenny was greeted inside by the waitresses
and cook. They acted like they knew her; probably let her use their
bathroom, knowing she occasionally bedded down in the ravine
across the street.

As we drove toward Jack's house, I waited for Callie to lob
a few more bombs my way. I assume she had been humiliated by
the scene.

"I never thought I would say this." Her voice was tired. "But I
think you should give up your search for a meaning to life, especially one through Christ. You should just admit, and I should accept,
that you believe there is no purpose to this life. This search has led
to nothing but disappointment for me and frustration for you. I
suppose some people are just not wired to believe there is a God."

"Talk about giving up the fort," I responded with a little
sharpness. "So I'm clumsy, but some people just have to stumble
along and stumble into believing. All of this business about grace
being handed out, well, hopefully there is grace, if there is such a
thing, for the stumblers."

Callie wasn't hearing any of that kind of excuse. "See, you can't even make a sentence about believing without putting a qualifier on it like, if there is such a thing. Really, Sonny, just be happy with the unhappy idea that there is nothing to this life."

Some moments, no matter how brief, can be so revealing that they define us. The drive through a buttery sunset was one of those. It was a defaming injury of the soul, where a hard light was cast on the basic me and found an empty room. I had hit bottom on this search for Jack. My wife had called me out of hiding. I had been trying to build a case for a purposeful existence out of a search for a man who never was—Jesus in his 60's. It was fool's gold I had mined, of no more substance than a daydream.

I said nothing to Callie as we drove to Habersham Road and Jack's expansive home. I was worn down and worn out.

Jack looked bad. Cancer is a taker. It can bleach the skin into chalk; leaves us careless about combing or being neat. Our minds and bodies relinquish to the angry march of the cells. Jack's face was taut, drained of the juices that plump us and give us a sheen and a glow. But he had his quick laugh. Death is not always an instant light switch. Some lights stoically stay on as others flicker and fade. He stood thinly, leaning slightly. The girls went on into the kitchen with the salmon and salad Callie had made.

"So what's this about a homeless woman coming to dinner?" He grinned. "Sounds like a joke on the girls."

I was shocked. "Who told you that?"

"Callie called Betty about what food to bring and told her you had thought about bringing this woman over, but then had a sudden attack of common sense and backed out."

I felt betrayed. Why did Callie have to say that? "I then responded, "Maybe it's a part of the message."

"What message?"

"The one you asked me to go and search for, you dope; the hunt for the parachute. I've found that you have to be careful what you search for, because you might find out things you don't want to know."

"So what the hell does bringing a homeless woman over here got to do with anything?" As weak as he was, Jack still had some fire in him.

"The invitation just came out in a parking lot when she was about to hit me up for money," I said, and then shrugged (I couldn't tell Jack that his best friends all had excuses about not coming, so I had asked her).

"Before we found that cross in the golf cart, I wouldn't have given her the time of day. Maybe I'm being led or being told something."

He put his hand on my shoulder and looked at me in a stern way. "Well, I'll tell you something. Don't bring people to my house that look like they never heard of a toothbrush, a comb, or saw a laundry. That's the message from me."

I was put out with that. "Damn it, I told you months ago I am the last man on the planet Earth to conduct a search for a savior for you. That's your job, not mine. You find him."

His hand clasped my shoulder harder. His eyes glistened. "Okay, I'm sorry. That was a little hard. But I can't find him. Since I found out I'm dying, I've tried every mental trick in the book. I've talked to Sandy and prayed with him. My heart just can't buy it. I need help and you're the only one I can believe. I know it's ridiculous, but you're my good messenger. Hell, bring a busload of the homeless over here, if that's what it takes."

I hugged him. We had never hugged. "I'm trying, Jack. Don't give up on me. But I may tell you this is it. No God. No way. No meaning. I've got to be honest, even if it's not what you want to hear."

"I can live with honesty, good or bad," Jack said, but not very convincingly, unless he had given in to oblivion being his destination.

It was a good evening, accented by stories of some of Jack's more theatrical courtroom antics. We laughed, Jack in short, timid bursts about golf and a trip a group of us had taken to England. Jack said, "Hey, you should have asked Max and Phil to come tonight. They took that trip with us. It was wild."

I couldn't say that they had all turned me down. "Oh, you'll see them at some point. We just wanted to have you by ourselves." I looked at Callie who wouldn't look at me because she knew I was lying. Even when it was a good and necessary lie, she hated it.

It was nine o'clock and he was noticeably tiring. "Hey, we need to get going. I'll get a bunch of the guys and we'll come over and drink your whiskey and tell lies."

"Bring your own damn whiskey along with your lies," Jack managed a last chuckle.

As the girls had their goodbye hugs, Jack grabbed my arm and whispered, "And bring me the message."

Looking for Love

The August sun would not release its hold. Humidity flowed in rivers of steam up from the Gulf, so Atlanta was a sauna. It was too hot to play golf except early in the morning, and then it was still too hot. I had gone over to the club's pro shop to leave my driver. While the assistant pro was putting a new grip on it, I thought I would take some laps in the pool. I was skipping lunch, hoping the workout and no calories would stop my gathering waistline.

"Hi, Sonny, when we going to work on your putting?" It was Dan Sims, The Creek's head pro and teacher. He could read the plane of your swing, the turn of your shoulders, the nuances of your grip, like an oracle. He could work on the mechanics of the body. But few pros can work on the mechanics of the mind. And that's where golf resides. So I had stopped taking lessons and started concentration exercises.

"Oh, by the way, Mr. Charlie Bradley asked if I saw you to tell you he'd be out by the pool." Dan looked out the window at the pool and said reflectively, "I swear I read he had been killed years ago. You know, that may not even be him."

I immediately felt annoyed. "Who is this guy, Dan? I know he was one of the club's founders, but what's his story?"

"That's a part of his myth. Charlie wasn't a founder. His mother was. The story goes that he wanted to turn their house, now this clubhouse, into a spiritual retreat. The Bradleys owned about two hundred acres here when Buckhead wasn't any more than a dirt road with a country store that had a buck's head on a pole in front of it. The family has sold the land to homeowners over the years. Tuxedo Road, Habersham, West Paces; all of these fancy streets with their big houses were created out of this land. That new money created a demand for a social club. The Bradley family was approached by women in the area to sell the house and use it for a club. Five hundred families put up $500 each and bought the house." Dan's arms were speckled in white, brown and darker spots. Hours of sunlight sun had christened his skin with discoloration.

"Charlie had been a stonemason and was said to be a damn good carpenter, all of which embarrassed his brothers and sisters who were doctors. He did small construction work until his early twenties when he just disappeared, left the country."

"An interesting story," I responded, but still felt there remained a mystery about this man.

"He's a lifetime member here because the original family got a membership as part of the sales agreement. He likes to eat lunch with people, and speaks in parables. Some of the men say he's a philosopher; others say he's trying to act like some Jesus character. Are ya'll friends?"

"Not at all. In fact, I think he's a little weird myself. I did speak with him briefly a few days ago. Couldn't see his face very well though. What's he sitting out in this heat for?"

"Weird, like you said, I guess. He's sitting over by the big fan so he hasn't totally lost it. Got a, what would you call it, an Arabian-looking robe on. Guess it's cooler than clothes."

"Crazy is the right adjective." A tall, older man, with a beak nose and small, sun-cracked lips, had walked up next to me, waiting to talk to Dan. Dan and I both looked at the man.

"I had heard he was killed years ago in the Middle East somewhere. Had made everybody in Buckhead mad when he was young.

The preachers couldn't stand him. He would stand on the steps at Dogwood Presbyterian and tell people coming in to go home and worship God by themselves. They didn't need the big church. Nobody would hire him to do repair work anymore, so he left the country. Seems he became a wandering spiritual guy. That man out there may be an imposter. I swear Charlie was killed before any of us were even born."

"So where does he live?" I asked both men.

"There's a tool shed on the back of this property that the family owns until the last of the original family dies. It was once a slave cabin. I suspect he's staying there." Dan explained.

I had journeyed a ways in the time since I practically told Charlie what to kiss. There was something very annoying about him, but he also had some kind of attraction that I couldn't fathom.

After putting my swim trunks on, I walked out into the bright. I had left my sunglasses at the office, so I squinted across the tiles toward the water. I could see him in the shade of a table umbrella. It was next to the pool and in front of a large fan that was breezing the pool. I jumped in the water. It was cool enough because the club had installed a water-cooling system after members complained the summer water was like swimming in pee. I took several laps, ignoring him on purpose. I could feel his presence and knew he was waiting for me, so I kicked to the corner; his table sat above. The water there was only three feet deep, so when I came out of the water I could reach and touch one of his chairs.

I thought I would show some restraint and respect. "We've got a really hot one today, huh?" The light of the day was so startling in its brightness that my eyes were rendered almost useless. They had retreated into bare slivers.

His voice was soft and slow, so each word was caressed and given its own life. Almost a song, but said not sung.

"Really hot? What is really? What is real?" He seemed amused. "At least we know the heat and the love of the Father is real."

I didn't answer. He had the same fedora hat on. I could see his nose was thick and protruded, but, again, his face was lost in the brim of the hat, and the shade was made darker because the sun was sterilizing, bleaching out everything it shined upon.

"That's quite a robe you've got on there. Looks like one of those Bedouin things," I finally responded. He had on a shoe length, cream-colored cotton robe.

"I lived among the Bedouins for years," he said. "This was what we wore. It makes nice pool wear. It was Georgia-hot over there, but they stay comfortable with these thin cotton coverings."

"So you played Lawrence of Arabia. What was that like?"

"It was life at its most simple; earth and heaven as one in their emptiness. Heaven envelops the desert at night. I wish we could gather all of the earth's people to lie on their backs each night in the Jordanian desert. There would be such a collective sighing and laughing and weeping in the realization of the oneness of it all."

I dwelled on his words for a moment then observed with regret, "Won't happen here. There is no night at night in Atlanta; too much ambient light. I understand that your family owned all of this land."

"All pastures and pine woods," he answered. "Buckhead was considered an escape from Atlanta. People would have cabins out here; then a few started estates."

I laughed with surprise. "This is six miles from downtown, and it was considered in the country?"

"Six miles was a lot longer in 1930 than it is today."

"I heard you were once pretty good with your hands; I mean with stone work and wood." I was trying to get him to reveal more about himself, even more, why he seemed to have an interest in me.

"Wood is like flesh or a liquid stopped in mid flow; like a stream suddenly stopped in all of its eddies and currents. I find peace in its touch. I feel like a sculptor when I work with it."

"Did you do that overseas?" I inquired.

I could hear him breathe in slowly, as though he were ruminating over what to say.

"I worked all around the Mediterranean. But I spent much of my time in observation and contemplation." He lingered on each word. And then he asked, "How is your search for the Son going?"

I bobbed in the water, keeping my body squatted down but my chin resting on the surface. "I assume you mean Jesus. How did you know about that?" I probably asked a little quickly and with an edge. He didn't know me from Adam, but he knew too much about me and how? Why?

"Oh, it's around the grill." He sounded bemused, as though I didn't know my friends had told their friends. Not like it was a secret.

"I know that your friend Jack is dying and that he wants, did he say, a 'parachute'? And he wants it with some desperation. Will your search reveal the answers that he needs in time?"

"It's been an eye opener," I answered. "I know facts about Jesus the man I never thought of. The Christ part may be a journey too far for me. But at least I'm on the trail."

"Gandhi said that men become what they imagine themselves to be. You imagine yourself to be guided by proof and facts and evidence that can be tested. Why not imagine that this life, this universe, is ultimately a mystery. Know that within that mystery is a reality. But to know it you have to have faith that the reality is there."

I stood up in the water. It was starting to dry my skin. My hands and fingers were wrinkling and white. I got out, put a towel

I had left on the side around my shoulders and pulled a chair away from the table and sat down. Fleeing from the sun, my pupils had reduced themselves to the size of a pencil's lead, making the dark under the umbrella a lingering cloak.

"What are your thoughts about Jack's coming death?" he asked. "What are your thoughts about death?"

I could have said, "Well, I'm dying right now in this heat," but that would have been my typical escape answer to a question I didn't want to dwell on. And my curiosity about Charlie made me more reflective.

I answered, "I've never witnessed an actual death. I was out of town when my father died suddenly. I've not been to that many funerals, mostly uncles and aunts. When you are younger, someone passing away seems normal when it's an older aunt or uncle. They were supposed to do that, to die. They were old and shuffled around and were colorless. Their deaths were quiet affairs in a stark, white-sheeted bed."

Memories filled me. "In their caskets they looked ashen but otherwise peaceful. Death was clean and quiet and respectful, filled with song and praises of lives led long and gracefully. It was all very neat and ordered. God was almost congratulated for bringing home such a wonderful person."

"And Jack, how do you feel about his passing?" he persisted.

"He may be the first person I actually witnessed passing away, and it is haunting and troubling; a real downer. And I will ask, why the misery? You don't hurt those you love. God's supposed to love us, so where's the love, God?" I asked rhetorically.

"Misery is part of the mystery. This is a free will world, and that opens the door for all kinds of suffering. Perhaps there is a reason we can't yet know." He sounded comfortable with what he had said.

I could feel a touch of anger and resentment and impatience. "You know, I'm really tired of this constant rationalizing about all of the suffering in this world by saying, 'Oh, God has a reason.' Baloney. What good reason is there for my friend Jack to be scared out of his wits about dying? His wife and children are crying all the time." I asked again, "Where's the love?"

He said nothing for a long while. We sat in the soft whirl of the large fan nearby.

"It's an understatement to say you are of little faith, Sonny. And I would say you can fight with God over why this and why not that, being always angry with him for not being Santa Claus. Or you can surrender your heart to The One and feel secure in that great love."

I countered his statement. "Or, I could say there is no God, so all the wars, deaths in the world, all of the love is for nothing, so just accept this world as without purpose. Here today, gone tomorrow, and who cares?" I added. "That's pretty depressing."

"That's why Jack is depressed. Most people want to think there is a reason we are on this earth. He feels…"

I interrupted, "He feels the lights will go out. No nothing. No dreamy place where he meets his loved ones and where everybody just yuks it up forever."

"You truly are cynical, or is it anger with Abba because he won't reveal himself according to your idea of proof of his existence and caring."

"Abba? Who's that?" I asked.

"Sorry, that's Aramaic for what you would call 'Daddy.'"

I really went off at him. "How about Abrakadabra? That's what all of this is, right? Aren't we just God's entertainment? His enjoyment in an otherwise extremely boring universe." The frustrations I had had with religion came out.

"Have you seen space?" I asked rhetorically. "It's empty; that why they call it space. I would create some little characters too, just for laughs. I'd say, 'Okay, people, have at it. Get stupid. Fight each other. Act like idiots, because you have brought humor to my very empty universe.'"

I stared at Charlie's revealing image. His face was relatively square with pronounced, almost chunked features; strong cheek-bones; thick, dark eyebrows; a square chin. There was an intensity about his eyes, but a tenderness about his mouth.

I realized I was being unusually free, having a heavy conversation with a man I didn't know. "We don't want to feel little, so to speak. We don't want to be a speck, a dust mote in the emptiness of space. I remember when that picture was taken on the moon of the earth sitting so small right over the moon's horizon. I had a friend who had to start seeing a psychiatrist it made him feel so insignificant."

Charlie sat quietly for a moment then said, "Significance. People are so self-inflicting in their wounds. They feel so inadequate and helpless. They tell themselves they must be noticed. They must feel significant. Looking up at the stars can make you feel like nothing. Or it can fill you with wonder that you are a part of such a creation."

"So my significance is that I am a part of something much larger and infinitely significant." I mused. "Well, I'm not sure being an important spec in an endless universe really makes me feel that important."

"That's because you can't let go of you. Do you want the Lord to appear here now so you could sense personally how mighty He is? Then wouldn't you feel like a puppet or scared to death of a presence so overwhelming it made you feel even more insignificant?"

Charlie continued, "There is a loving God who can and does intercede, but with no regularity. Free will is the driving force that was created to run the universe, and that free will is kept sacred with every war, every car wreck, every birth and love story, all of the ebbs and flows of life."

We were butting heads over this, so I let it drop. I wanted to know more about his time in the Middle East, so I said. "Let me ask you this. Since you have heard of my researching Jesus, did your studies or contemplation as you said, reveal anything about him as a man?"

He took a long drink from a glass of what looked like water. "Jesus was born into a scarred but resilient land. I found Galilee a fertile place of swells for hills, separated by small plains and watered almost exclusively by springs. In the time of Jesus the roads were ankle-twisters strewn with all manner of rocks and sided by cactus that loves to catch your clothes; but very fertile. Jesus would have had a healthy vegetarian diet."

"No meat. No T-bone steaks?" I asked facetiously.

"Think about it. They didn't have refrigeration. If you killed a cow or bull, you had to eat it then. So, yes, he would have eaten beef, but only at a large wedding or festival. And then probably on a shish kabob."

"They had sheep, so probably some lamb and goat."

"Sheep were more for wool; goats for their meat, milk and cheese, and goat skin for tents. But yes, Jesus would have had those meats on occasion. But a lot of fruit, olives and figs, and many kinds of vegetables."

"How about *The Jesus Diet*, now at your bookstore." I injected.

"Don't laugh. That whole Mediterranean region ate very healthy," Charlie replied.

"So what caused you to go overseas in the first place?" I continued to try and draw him out, in part to discover why he had an interest in me.

"I felt I was surrounded by hypocrites here. They were good people, very generous and caring, but they sought God in the shallowness of churches and religion. I made too many of my family's friends angry. I was very confrontational after I committed my life to my real father."

"You mean God?" I assumed.

"I don't use the name God. I call him One, Father, Blessed, or, as you now know, Abba." His voice sounded almost cheery in the soft drawl he had been speaking in.

I persisted, "Why the name of One? And why do we have a God that has no name? I always thought that strange; it makes him more abstract."

"In that regard we are similar to the Chinese philosophy of Tao. It says the universal force (they called it 'The Way') had to be nameless. It is so unfathomable, so out of our realm of understanding, that it can have no name. When you give anything a name, you have defined it." Charlie's depth of knowledge seemed endless.

"But I called God One because I wanted to be one with the Father. I wanted to be the early Adam again. Could I be sinless, I would ask myself. Could I give all my life to my new father? Not in Atlanta I couldn't. I had to strip myself of myself, and the only way I knew how to do it was to go where the geography was both brutal and sacred."

"So you headed for the Holy Land," I surmised.

"To the wilderness, into the great emptiness across the Jordan River where I would stay for forty days."

I was always doubtful about how Jesus the human could have survived forty days without water or even food. "So you loaded up with Coppertone, a big straw hat, a nice tent from North Face and jugs of Evian. And Pizza Hut promised deliveries weekly. But to get into the John the Baptist official wilderness experience you did try a locust or two."

His voice suddenly sounded dismayed. "Your friend Jack may have chosen the wrong explorer."

I realized I was getting a little too flip. "No doubt about that. This explorer is very lost," I concurred.

"And that may be the first step to finding what you seek. I became committed to our Lord as a child. My father was pure in his belief, and this had enormous influence on me. I tried becoming totally committed to my faith. But, I knew I couldn't do it in Buckhead." He breathed in deeply, as if to summon more of his thoughts.

"I became confrontational and angry, because I saw our version of Christianity as basically a social, feel-good affair. I felt my friends and my family's friends didn't have in mind the things of God, but the things of men. I was also angry with myself because as I criticized others, I realized I was not really carrying the cross either."

"I've never approached a level of faith that I didn't think was even adequate to get to heaven." This man had been a mile ahead of me, and he thought he was failing at faith.

He ignored my remark. "I was too worried over my cabinet and stone work. I obsessed over making each plank cut to be the perfect cut. Each stone mortared to another stone must be the perfect match. But I wasn't seeking perfection as a spiritual man. I was after the wrong glory."

I waved for a waiter who was serving the pool to bring me a Virgin Mary. Charlie got a chuckle out of that, mumbling to himself, "Very appropriate. That's a salvation plan; joke your way into

heaven. Make God laugh so hard he won't notice your sneaking in."
He was amused with his musings.

"There's that song, 'Been looking for love in all the wrong
places', I could transpose God for love. But I've been trying to find
God, I now know, the only way my logical mind could, and that's
to know the real Jesus; the one who walked around as a man."

"Sonny, you may be looking too hard. You have filled yourself with so much information you may have become ignorant. You
have filled your cup so full, it's empty."

"Charlie," I said in my defense, "I knew little about Jesus. I
had to start somewhere. I couldn't just say 'Okay, I think I'll just
give my Life to Jesus.' And, Shazaam, I'm a true believer. By the
way, how did you survive the forty days?" I changed the subject.

"I had food to eat that you, explorer, know nothing about.
My mind began to feed me after a few days. I took no water. Only
the clothes I wore. I tested myself against the temptations I knew
would come from hunger. I believed life was more than food, and
my body more than clothing. And I knew that worrying over these
things would not add a single hour to my life."

I objected, "Sorry, but a human can't live that long with no
water or in that sun that long."

"I was provided water in the morning dew on cactus leaves,
and a dripping spring out of a rock. In a small cave I curled up like a
happy dog. And I did eat locust and scorpions, without the stingers.
My mind emptied painfully and slowly during those days. Barren
land and immense skies have that effect. I gained a great singularity
of clarity."

"After the forty days what did you do?" I was fascinated by
his story.

"I lived with the Bedouin for several years. We camped with
many different caravans, and I got to know a range of people and

beliefs. But I wanted to continue the simplest life in which I could survive. I traveled to Egypt where I lived in a monastery at Wadi El Natruon. It is where the ancient Egyptians dug sodium bicarbonate for embalming. It is believed by some that Joseph brought his family here when they escaped from Herod's killing of children."

Charlie and his life were a million miles from my cloistered world. His knowledge was all encompassing. "Three hundred years after the death of Christ," Charlie continued, "a number of Christians wanted to escape from Roman culture and persecution, so they went to this northern Egyptian desert and lived as hermits. They became known as the Desert Fathers, and their life of humility, solitude and prayer had enormous influence on Christian theology."

"Charlie, every one I've interviewed makes me feel how shallow my Christianity has been. I don't know beans about the history of this faith or the man who founded it."

"I will challenge you, Sonny. Just how committed are you willing to become? Hear the words of a monk, Blessed Macarius, from that period who said, 'This is the truth; if a monk regards contempt as praise, poverty as riches, and hunger as a feast, he will never die.'"

The tomato juice over ice with Tabasco sauce and pepper was delivered. It was thick and cold and refreshing. The words of poverty as riches and this cold tomato juice were a thousand miles apart.

"My journey may be stalled out," I said with resignation, after a sip. "That kind of thinking is not just foreign to me, it makes me believe Christianity is more about seeing how you can beat yourself down as much as be uplifting. I'm not sure I'm made to be a Christian. It's almost antihuman."

"Maybe so. Maybe you are forever stranded in your own wilderness of the soul. You're a logical, orderly thinker. I want you to see if you can meet with an evolutionist out at Fernbank Museum by the name of Abraham Sears. Called Abby. His father and I exchanged letters years ago. He was an amateur archeologist and wanted to do some digging outside Jerusalem and wanted to know if I would assist. I did, and we became friends. But I don't think Abby would remember me. He was a child."

"So why are you recommending him?" I asked.

"I've read a lot about him. He's a darling of the Atlanta papers. Always finding some million-year-old fossil or ancient Indian village. Abby is an atheist. You have been informing yourself with believers and yet you remain uncertain. Maybe if you talked with a very bright man who is convinced God does not exist you at least can find comfort in knowing in your heart that there is no purpose to us, no heavenly father. And this news you can take to Jack."

"Charlie, let's get real. I don't care how close you get, God is not your Father. Your father was your father. I mean, how far do we take this father business? At what point does religion become play-like and when is it real?"

I was pushing Charlie, I could tell, because the sweetness and caring in his voice abruptly modulated to an undercurrent of exasperation. "There's no play-like going on when one has opened his heart to the Holy Spirit. That is reality. God is the original Father of us all. Our earthly fathers simply passed along what God put in them to pass along. They are merely vessels. But they are expected to be as The Father, caring and loving of what they have created."

"Sorry, but the daddy that raised me is John McGrath."

"You're finding, as was said, Sonny, that the gate is narrow and the way is hard to the Father's Kingdom."

"I find that statement disappointing and an indictment of a narrow-minded God. Why the necessity of being endlessly tested? Why let in so few? God gave us passions, and then he gets mad when we use them. It all seems like a very cruel game."

"I have found it revealing," Charlie said, "that suffering seems to bring us closer to God. Suffering must be an essential part of God's plan."

I could tell this conversation with this very strange man was coming to an end. He had reached a level of belief that was as distant as another continent to me. He even sounded like Jesus. But it was a state of mind, like a brass ring I felt I might be forever reaching for. After this conversation I felt the whole endeavor to find out more about life's meaning through Jesus the man was looking like a waste of time. But I would at least get a retirement idea out of Charlie.

"Since you apparently overheard me talking about what Jesus would have done had he lived into his 60's, what do you think? Maybe he would have gone to Egypt and led the life of one of those Desert Fathers you spoke of?"

He said nothing for a long moment. I thought he was going to ignore the question. And he did.

Interesting, he wouldn't answer my question. Insulted? Too blasphemous for him? Too absurd? Charlie wasn't moving from his chair, and I needed to get to work. I stood and walked out from the table, back into the glare and asked, "Charlie, I don't believe my returning a necklace is the reason you seem to have sought me out. What's this all been about?"

He then responded quickly. "I've always favored the phrase 'living waters'. Our lives are living waters whose courses can be changed by a word, an event, a look, a smile. I was curious if my leaving the cross in the golf cart, as simple as it was, would alter anyone's path."

I nodded. "I figured as much. It was a little too obvious, but it worked in one respect."

Then he sounded pleased, "It started you on a search for a man you have never really known. I overheard you and your friends in the grill some time back discussing it. I knew that the bracelet had opened the door, and you walked through it."

Under his fedora his hair was full and dark and almost to his shoulders. I thought it odd that a man in his eighties would have hair so luxuriant and with color. "Was it your wife's bracelet?"

"No. I was never blessed with a wife. I left Atlanta so young, and at that time my spiritual growth precluded the care and nurturing a wife would deserve. I found that bracelet on the lowest day of my forty days, in the emptiness of the Jordanian desert. I spent the first week moving among the dry streambeds and their overhanging banks. From the first day the sun was a threat to my life. Shade was my salvation. At my weakest point, with little water and no food, I prayed mightily, not for those things, but for a spot where the sun could no longer tempt me to leave the desert."

"Haven't I read this story before? A man goes into a suffering place called the wilderness and the Devil tempts him," I prodded.

He ignored that sophomoric alluding to Jesus. "I was terrified that the temptations would overwhelm me and send me running for help. I was staggering along a small hill, having been burned badly by the sun, when I heard the jangle of bells and saw the approach of several camels and their riders. They were Bedouin tribesmen on the way to trade some splendid knives they had made to barter for goods they needed.

They gave me water and figs and bread, and a square of goatskin for a tent. The tent was a miserable sheet of skin, but it rendered the sun powerless. I still have that little tent. And one of them gave me the little cross that you found. That was many years ago."

I sat back down under the umbrella. The sun's rays were a rain of stingers. "I've thought many times of doing some wilderness thing. You know, go out to Glacier Park and just sit and stare at the incredible scenery. Kind of a commune-with-nature weekend. But I've often wondered after staring at the beauty of the valleys and jagged peaks for a while; what in the world do you think about all day?"

"You don't go to the full. You go to the empty, to the barren."

"Sounds boring as hell." I thought a second then concluded, "If hell is boring."

He ignored my commentary on hell. "The purpose of losing yourself is to purge the mind of possessions that you treasure. It's been called Christian mysticism. The purpose is to see if you can embrace the treasure of the spiritual world, becoming one with God through contemplation and deep prayer. I suspect you haven't lost enough to free yourself."

"No disrespect," I countered, "but sitting out in the middle of nothing with no food would make me think of a cold beer and a hamburger. Seriously, Charlie, The Lord gave us a mind, a questioning, critical, show-me-the-money mind, so I don't see why some of us can't think our way to heaven."

"Read John Polkinghorne for one. Some very, very bright people have studied this creation and concluded that it is God-created. And this path seems to be the one you are journeying on. I also think you are in what St John of the Cross in the 1500's called 'the dark night of the soul.'"

"And that is?"

"To you that means the struggle you are going through, the darkness; to find, not a carpenter, but a Savior."

I stood again. It was late. I had to go to work. "Charlie, I appreciate your interest in me. The bracelet gimmick worked. It has led me down a road that's more than a study of retiring, but to being a reluctant, spiritual helper for a dying friend. But we're all dying, Charlie, and I have found I need a helper as badly as he does."

"I tell you that He is with you now as we speak. He sits before you in me." Holding his arms out, he said, "The Love reaches out to you with an affection that you have never known; if you will only have the eyes to see and the ears to hear the word."

I slipped my feet into my sandals and said with some dejection, "My eyes are blind to this, Charlie, and my ears are deaf. And I'm truly sorry to say that."

He said, "Then go and visit Abby and at least know the truth that is true for you. Goodbye, son."

What's the point of my continuing to sit on the fence, I wondered. I've spoken with some brilliant people who have intensely studied this and found meaning in life through Christ. And after all of that I'm still not swept up in some spiritual awakening. I just don't feel it. And by the way, what is *It*?

I left the pool feeling very down and still somewhat confused about Charlie and exactly who he was. But he had gotten into me in a strange way. It seemed my search for Jack had become a study in failure by me of me. I was in an emotional freefall.

God's Funeral

This was the last interview I was going to do. The whole process had beaten me down. I had always thought of myself as comfortably Christian. After this journey I know what that means. It means being basically a good person as defined by me, which means giving to various charities in painless amounts, and being active on several church committees. I now know that I, and many of my friends, have taken the basic ingredients of Christianity and designed our own religion from that. I also know that religion served my deep down fear of oblivion; Jesus covered up that chilling fear very well.

The interviews had exposed my entire religious facade. Jack knew I was a faker. That's why he demanded I find myself out. It was like, in his final days, he wanted me to discover myself, not just to find if there's any life after death for him. I had failed all the little tests that had been put before me in the interviews. I sold out every value I thought I had at the least temptation.

My wife had seen through the veil I erected. She had called me out as being a pretender. She and this strange man Charlie had both given up on my finding any purpose to life. Feeling I had no redeeming values, and knowing I had lied to myself and those around me about what I truly believed, I prepared to go and hear my new high priest, an avowed atheist. I would listen to his wisdom and leave cleansed of my lies and accepting of my new faith that said our lives are as empty as shadows. I went to him as an emptied container.

The summer of 2010 was a succession of 90-degree days. It was especially oppressive on this day in middle Georgia, south of Macon. The site was on a deer-hunting preserve that was populated by pine trees in all of their thinness, with a lonely oak here and there left, I suppose, by land-stripping cotton farmers as a shade oasis for their field hands.

Much of the land is briar swirls and a profusion of grasses and bushes beseeching the sandy and depleted soil for some nourishment. Cotton feasted on it years ago and has left enough open spaces for deer to thrive.

I drove off the main highway down a sandy path begging fruitlessly to be called a road to a log house. This was the meeting place for the invited deer hunters during that season. Now it served as a starting place for the Fernbank excavation crew. Following Abby's instructions, I parked and walked off down a trail toward where I heard voices.

I soon came into a clearing where the narrow Ocmulgee River flowed before me. Soil had bled into the river until it was a light chocolate color. The river at this place was without any character that would make one sit and admire it. I saw people off to my right.

Standing on a small beach and facing a large exposed sandy bank was a thin man in a broad-rimmed straw hat. He was talking to four young people who were on their knees, scrapping into the bank with trowels. As I walked up, he turned and said, "Mr. Charlie's friend, I presume?"

I joked back at his allusion to the famous Stanley and Livingston encounter. "Mr. Livings…uh, Mr. Cole I assume. And, yes, Mr. Charlie said we should meet."

We shook hands then he reached down, picked up a trowel and handed it to me. With a broad grin that crinkled his tanned face, he said, "Before we discuss what brings you here, let me hand you your personal time machine. It will take you back to 32 million BC in just a few scoops."

I took the trowel and looked at him in disbelief. "No way that bank is that old."

"Sure is. This was the edge of the ocean at that time, and this is where deer or hippos turned into whales and became aquatic creatures."

"I had heard that, but how do you know that? Some people feel that evolution is a threat to their religion. They say there is no fossil proof of animals moving from one species to another."

He frowned underneath the straw hat from which the imperfect weaving was speckling his face with smatterings of sunlight. "I assume you mean Christians? Who cares what they say?" he responded dismissively. "Whales have become the new standard for proving that life can and did evolve from one species to another. Look here."

He motioned for me to look at several pieces of dull white bone sticking out of the bank. One of the students stood and moved and Abby pointed at a circular shape at one end of a tooth-filled jawbone.

"This is an example of the ear bone of a land animal in transition to becoming sea-based. The bone has shifted for directional hearing underwater, though it has not fully finished evolving. These changes gradually evolved, and we also have examples of the pelvis and legs in various stages of evolving."

He took his hat off, revealing a smallish, square face, peeling in tiny skin twirls from a recent sunburn. His eyes were friendly but squinted, as though they were appraising you. There was a slightness about his build, but not delicate at all, as he stood with an obvious firmness. This kind of constant outside work demanded enormous durability and stamina.

Abby stepped away and looked at me. "If you're a believer, you would have to say your God was extremely deliberate, a very slow mover. He has created a free will world where life moves at its own speed according to the pressures put on it by weather, available food and competition."

"Listen, I want to thank you for allowing me to come out here. I know paleontology is not about understanding God, but about understanding ancient animals."

"That's true, but I was intrigued by your call when you said Charlie Bradley had recommended I see you. I was born near his family's home. He was kind of legendary in Buckhead; initially a confrontational, spiritual teenager who would stand at the local churches and tell members to go home and find God. He was like a John the Baptist character. The next thing anybody knew he went to some desert and became a cross between Lawrence of Arabia and kind of a Jesus twin."

I chuckled, "That's a strange combination."

"What's stranger is that I swear that man died when I was about ten. It was written up in the paper. It was the talk for a while. Killed just outside of Jerusalem near where Jesus was supposed to have been crucified. I still remember it and that was 50 years ago."

"Then I've been talking to a ghost or an impersonator."

"Obviously he really wasn't killed, and it did intrigue me enough to agree to have you come on out. We have to be a little careful who we let know about what we're up to because locals will loot these digs in a heart beat."

A mosquito that looked like a toy helicopter made its soft decent onto my hand that was holding the trowel. "Damn! Look at the size of that thing," I exclaimed, as I slapped it into a smear.

"I also thought it strange," Abby admitted, "that you wanted to talk to me about the historical Jesus. In your email you said

Charlie told you I was an atheist, which is true. So why seek me out?"

"Some retired golfing buddies and I were speculating on what Jesus could have been like as an older man. I thought I would ask around for the heck of it and report back. But it's turned into more than that. It's become more a journey to find out where I really stand on believing in the God of the Bible or any god. You know, the old 'what's it all about thing.'"

"Sounds like Jesus described you in John, 'You have never heard his voice nor seen his form, nor does his word dwell in you, for you do not believe the one he sent.'"

I'm sure the surprise showed on my face that this atheist was quoting the gospels and accurately describing me.

"Surprised that I know more scripture than you? Don't be. Most atheists I know became one after much study and thought. We know the Bible better than most Christians."

He situated his straw hat back on again, recasting his face in light speckles. "Where do you stand?" He asked pointedly.

The abruptness startled me. I didn't know him and found his question to be bordering on a confrontation. I simply said, "Lost. That's where I am. Charlie felt I couldn't accept that Christ was real, or that there was any meaning to be found in any religion. He felt if I heard the rationale of an atheist, I might go ahead and accept that I was an atheist and if I am, then live with it."

Obviously put out, he asked angrily, "Am I on an archeological dig, or is this a retreat for lost souls? So what am I supposed to do? Convince you that there is no god? I'm not in that business. You are not here to attend God's funeral. It is a solitary event for each of us as the idea of God dies in each of us. Like the tooth fairy. But I don't try and create non-believing disciples. So you may want to save yourself some mosquito bites and poison ivy rash and head on back to Atlanta."

"No, no, it's not that. I'm not trying to be convinced. I'm really just gathering information from a scientist, a man who makes his living gathering evidence and testing it for its truth. I assume you did this in pursuing the reality of a god and concluded there is none. Just a couple of questions and I'll get out of your way."

Looking down at the sand, he pushed the toe of his boot over it as though he was thinking about what to do with this interloper that was interfering with his work. Then he seemed to calm down a bit, but still had an annoyed look. "Did you see the movie Avatar?"

I thought that an odd question. "Yeah. Seems like God and nature were one, or nature was God. Pantheism, I think it's called. It tolerates the possibility of many gods."

"You could say nature is god-like, not a god, as we think of gods. A force, if it must have a name. A rabbi asked Einstein if he believed in God and he wrote back, 'I believe in Spinoza's god who reveals himself in the orderly harmony of what exists, not in a god who concerns himself with the fates and actions of human beings.'"

"Spinoza?" I blurted out.

"Damn. Charlie should have told you to take a hike from the get go. You should have at least done some basic reading on what the major thinkers have said about religion. Baruch Spinoza was a Dutch philosopher in the 1600's who was one of the pioneers in modern rational thinking. He believed there was no inherent good or evil. We create these qualities because we don't understand the causes of various events. The pursuit of knowledge and the truths it unfolds should be man's highest goal."

"And you would subscribe to that?" I ventured.

"I do. That's why I study evolution on the one hand and ancient societies on the other. I'm insatiably curious about how we came to be."

"Some Christians criticize scientists as being so closed-minded about the possibility of a spiritual world that they have made science a religion." I was afraid I might be pushing what seemed a volatile and impatient personality.

His response was immediate. "That's pure baloney, and typical of what you hear from the intellectually challenged, otherwise known as religious people. Most of them think evolution is a threat to God's omnipotence."

"Since you don't believe in God, I assume you see evolution as the driving force behind the complexity of life?"

"That's what is going on, only it isn't being driven by any gods, but by the inalterable fact that when cells divide, they don't always turn into the cells they were supposed to. There are mutations, mistakes, and these lead to grass and giraffes and people evolving."

My coming here was a stupid idea; an imposition on a man content in who he is with no desire to convince others. But I had driven 90 miles to get here. I suggested a change of discussion. "So what if we forget the god stuff and I lend a hand on that deer turning into a whale?"

He smiled thinly, which broke his intensity, and he said with some comity, "One of the kids is out today. We could use a hand, but I gotta tell you he's out because he got into some poison ivy roots, and we had to take him to the emergency room in Macon. The roots are really toxic. Oh, and fire ants come down the roots looking for water."

"Hey, I don't remember Indiana Jones running into fire ants, poison ivy and helicopter-sized mosquitoes…anything else?"

"Yeah. Rattlesnakes are up on top of the bank. Killed a five footer yesterday."

"Look, I'm just a pilgrim searching for Jesus. Maybe I should search for him on my boat up at the lake."

"Then you might be asked to walk on water, and with no more faith than you have you'd drown."

I liked Abby. He didn't know me from anybody, had no need to give me a second of his time, but as quick-tempered as he seemed, I felt we were starting some kind of bonding based on humor, which is usually the way men relate. We're great at insulting one another as a part of the dance to see if we're compatible.

"All right, show me what to do here." I requested.

Going on a dig for fossils is one of those romantic notions, like wanting to own a bed and breakfast, a neat little restaurant, or wine shop. The nicest thing that can be said is that they are illuminating experiences. The truth, though, is these 'Oh, wouldn't that be fun' dreams are more often humiliating, exhausting forays into financial or mental ruin.

On this August day the sun had a merciless intensity, the horse flies and their smaller cousins, the mosquito, sought a breakfast of my blood, and the fire ants came bearing gifts of poison. With my time machine trowel I had entered my own purgatory. So this could be hell, my mind imagined, as I dug into the hardened limestone bank, a billion years of bites. It was enough to make me a Christian and seek the temperate climate, the green fields and buffet tables I imagined heaven to offer.

I said over my shoulder, now wet with sweat, "Abby, I think I am now ready to make that commitment to heaven."

He was bent over a table with a topographic map of the dig site. Without looking up, he answered, "Oh, yeah? Is that because you've arrived at hell's half acre?"

I dug at the bank for about an hour. My arms were covered in sweat-stuck sand. My eyebrows were like small water fountains constantly filtering the sweat from my forehead. The sun was focused angrily along the entire bank we were working. And then a dull sound.

"Whoa!" I was startled when my trowel hit something. I was digging down along the backbone of the whale, sliding my trowel carefully so as not to scratch the exposed bone.

Abby quickly came over. "What 'cha got?"

"The point of my trowel hit something, and it didn't feel like a rock."

He had a smaller trowel and a brush and began making meticulous probes into the depression I had dug. "Time for the surgeon to take over."

It wasn't long before he whispered, "We got it." He then looked at the crew working nearby and shouted with unmistakable joy. "Unbelievable! We've got a pelvis in transition."

The young crew rushed over as he pointed out what looked like another bone to me. I stood back, feeling elated that whatever it was, I had found it.

"Hey, guys, give some credit to the new paleontologist," I kidded. "Why don't we call this thing a Sonnysaurus?"

Abby's face went stern again. Taking my arm, he guided me slightly away from the kids that were now busily dusting dirt away from the bone. "First of all, it's not a lizard, it's a mammal, so there's no 'saurus' in the name."

"Well, what did I find?" I felt like a kid saying 'Look at me,' in front of some adults.

Abby was in my face and adamant. "Listen, forget you, and forget what you found. Your strutting around about making a major find can create a bad situation between my team and me. This opportunity is precious to them. They may never find an excavation where meaningful discoveries can be made for years. Your finding that pelvis can be very disheartening to them and make them resentful of me."

I felt both deflated and confused. "Why resentful of you?"

"Because I allowed some stranger to just walk on our site and find what they would have talked about for the rest of their career."

The students had completed uncovering what looked like a pelvis with a tiny leg attached to it. Abby announced, "This is a prime example of a species transitioning into another very different species. In order to become fully aquatic, these mammals had to shift their pelvis from being a walker to being a swimmer. Along with this the legs had become far smaller and were turning into fins. Good work, team," he said as he looked at them with his back to me. While the students continued to dig excitedly, really joyfully, Abby turned back to me.

"Wasn't it Darwin that said God does work in strange and wondrous ways?" I asked.

Abby pushed his hat back. "If you believe in myths, yes, he does. If you don't, then you see the power of natural selection where our bodies transform us to better survive in changing environments."

"So we are little gods."

He took his hat off, went over to his broad worktable and picked up a camera. "That may be a stretch, but you could say we are godlike. We create, we destroy, we love, kill, help, hurt. You can pray to us to do things you wish, and we can ignore or answer them. You can worship us. Yeah, we're kind of godlike."

One of the student diggers had cleared away more of the hardened sand so that the pelvis and little leg stood out clearly.

"Let's get pictures of us; then we'll get the scientific stuff within the grids. Got to make this official for other scientists to scrutinize." Abby set the camera up on a tri-pod and asked me to click the camera for photos of his group, then one was taken of himself and the pelvis. That would be the one for the scientific journals. I was put out that he didn't volunteer to take a picture of me. I found the damn thing.

"Is this really a major discovery?" I asked, again like a star-struck kid.

"To find this in Georgia it is, but these transitional animals have been found by the hundreds in the Sahara." He motioned for me to step aside while the students took more pictures.

Abby looked at his watch and announced. "Ten o'clock. Water and shade break."

He motioned for me to sit on a log with him while the other four lay under a tree next to the river.

I felt I needed to be honest with him. "Okay. I see your situation. Sorry about drawing attention to myself. I just want you to know I'm taking credit for nothing. You all had already unearthed that thing. I just pushed some dirt aside."

He looked at me intently. His face even discovered some understanding. "That's kind of you to say that. For somebody to just walk on the site and find something significant takes the wind out of the sails of these kids. They are all seniors from the University of Georgia and sadly they won't find many jobs like this. Getting funding for excavations is extremely hard to do."

"So what'll happen to them?"

"Go to work for a museum moving boxes of bones around. Work for a state Department of Transportation or an environmental company. But from-the-ground-up projects like this, they die for these jobs."

I drew a cup full of water from a big round orange water cooler sitting next to us, then said, "Speaking of dead things, let's go back to dying."

Abby laughed. "Uh, oh, here we go. What does the atheist think of his impending doom? Is he afraid of death? Will he have a deathbed confession? Save me, Jesus. Don't let me spend the next billion years tied to an ant hill on the Ocmulgee in August."

I liked his easy wit. I thought it was healthy, though very sarcastic. My wife would have gone back to the car, fulminating over this kind of trash talk about the Savior. I saw it as an opening to broach the subject I had come here for. "Let's get to it; why do you reject Christ?"

His face looked meditative. "My childhood upbringing in the Methodist church still makes me feel a tinge of darkness flowing over me when I hear a question like that."

"Maybe the spark is still there somewhere," I offered.

"No, I evolved, no pun intended, from being raised in the church and believing that Jesus was God to it slowly ebbing away. I transitioned like that whale over there and my mind and logic and study led me away to another spirituality."

I gave him a quick summary of how I viewed all of this. "You quoted Einstein. I read that he was humbled by the infinitely superior spirit that created the universe. I have always been interested in this whole God subject from different angles. My logical mind that said there is no God is also logical enough to say there may be something, a force, 'an intelligence of some kind', as Einstein said, but I'm struggling to see it."

"So what's this all about?" he asked. He shook his head softly; a wry smile crept over his face as though he had been visited by the question many times.

Then he answered himself. "You will find this ironical. I have found that in the story of this universe are quotes from Genesis and the Gospel of John. 'Now the earth was formless and empty, darkness was over the surface of the deep,' and then in John, 'In the beginning was the Word, and the Word was with God, and the Word was God.'"

"Wait a minute," I interjected. "You don't believe in God, but you believe the answer to what this universe is all about is in God's word."

He laughed. "Well, not exactly. I just find such poetry and accuracy in these scriptures. I like the phrase, 'Darkness was over the surface of the deep.' Before the universe was created there was darkness over the emptiness in all of its deepness, though some scientists argue there was no space. There was no nothing."

"No nothing. This stuff gets like some Alice in Wonderland story. Especially, and I have done a lot of reading about this, when you get to the quantum level where things really get crazy." I had been fascinated with all sciences since I was a kid.

"Yeah, in the littlest pieces that we can slice and dice matter, there seems to be vibrating strings of energy. Maybe," he said with equivocation.

"So you and I, all matter, is basically cooled down, congealed energy. That's not very comforting," I observed facetiously and half truthfully.

"And wanting to feel comfortable is exactly why men seek out gods. Men need comforting. Once consciousness entered our minds and we were aware of deep sadness and we could wonder, then we became vulnerable. We could feel vulnerability and fear of the unknown. The unknown became a fearsome force that threatened us."

"You're saying we needed a big brother to love and comfort and to kick ass and take names."

He drank long from a thermos and said, "And that big brother became a whole host of big sisters and brothers who were called gods. Every last civilization worshiped something. Later for Jews it became one god. God filled a desperate need to survive forever and be cared for. And that's a price you might say we pay for evolution."

"What do you mean a price to pay?" I queried.

Abby looked at his watch. The students were already back at work. "I had over two hundred applicants for these four jobs. These kids are so grateful and love paleontology so much, I have to make them take breaks and quit at six o'clock."

He continued, "I mean life forms evolve in those ways that make them safe and sustainable. There is a life imperative. All life has this yearning, if you will, to survive. Evolution allowed man to become cognitive and have smarts, but the price paid was to worry and have fear, especially of life ending."

"So this angst was a price of being smart."

"I believe religion became a glue, a common bond that made those tribes that believed stronger, more orderly and respectful than those that didn't. So the imperative to survive was satisfied through worship and reliance on greater powers."

"Which sounds like we made the whole God thing up to make us feel more comfortable in what you could argue is a very brutal reality, and that is we are the pointless result of a pointless mass of squiggly energy strings. This could get depressing." I'm sure I sounded depressed.

"But here's the key to the universe, I believe, as I quoted in John, whether you believe in God or not. 'In the beginning was the Word.' The word is another way of saying information. This universe is driven by exchanges of information from the level of particles all the way up to the complexity of our brains."

"That's something I have never understood. Nitrogen, hydrogen, carbon and all the other elements that make up life, are by themselves lifeless. They don't possess a consciousness. Why is it that just because they come together they have the ability to pass information around, as you say?" I asked.

He said. "Couldn't you say that about a computer? It stores and passes along information and it's made up of inanimate wiring. Or crystallization repeats itself."

I disagreed with his comparison. "That answer doesn't work for me. Plus, how did these no-brainer atoms start up life that replicated itself and eventually created brainiacs, massive information centers, like us, unless God created it."

Abby stood and stretched his legs. "I can't answer that. Maybe God did do it," he teased. "No, you're getting into the area which Rene Descartes in the 1600's proposed. And that was if you could describe all of the qualities of God and he had those qualities, then he must exist or you could not have described them."

"I don't buy that either," I countered. "But because of the intractable mystery of much of our universe, can't one logically conclude there is God? Not through testing, not through empirical evidence, but through a process of elimination of all other causes?"

"Sure, if you want to say just because we don't understand gravity then God must have made it. That's pretty weak. So what happens when we discover just what gravity is? Does than mean we take away another rationale for God?"

I stood up and could feel a slight stiffness in my lower back. "That's the slow death of God through the attrition of knowledge."

"Like the tide against a sand castle. God is in the mystery to many. But true believers either don't see mystery anywhere or they revel in the mystery. They are totally convinced a loving God is a fully explained reality."

We both smiled. "I'm intrigued by your knowledge and admiration of scripture," I said.

He leaned over and emptied a paper cup of water over his head, shook the water loose, then placed his broad-brimmed straw hat back on.

"I love the poetry of the Bible. It's a wonderful guide for living a sharing, loving life. It offers hope and comfort to us poor little creatures that are so in need of both."

"Before you say it, I know where this is heading," I said. "You're going to say next that all of these qualities fit perfectly into evolution. The pain of awareness of our pains was so great that we invited a medicine called God to take the pains away."

He slapped his leg in an exuberant agreement. "A deductive thinker has arrived at our little dig! You've got it. We pay a price for the complexity of our brains and that is fear, powerlessness and depression, if we think this thing called life is pointless. Interesting that we got so smart we got sad."

"I came here to get off the fence one way or another, Abby. I've struggled with these things all my life. And everything you've said makes perfect sense to me."

"I think I hear a big 'but' about to be expressed." He was very perceptive. "I'm afraid you have not come over to the dark side yet."

"Oh, I could argue that your convictions are the enlightened side. I see no darkness there. But maybe I'm too much of a romantic, scared of a world with no reason. I remain solid in my position on the fence."

"I could say that's a wasted position. You win no points from either side on that. If there were a God, he would kick your butt off to the non-believers side with whatever punishment that would entail. Since in my opinion there is no God of the Bible, there is no purpose to any of this, so you can sit wherever you want to, and it won't matter in the greater scheme of things."

I felt what beliefs I did hold were being verbally stoned. Were the Christian hopes I had no more than sandcastles, easy subjects to an angry tide of reason? I liked this atheist and realized I was vulnerable to his opinions.

"Abby, I've had this same conversation with myself many times, but not articulated like you do it. I need to admit that all religions are myths with no more validity than campfire ghost stories. That's probably where this whole notion of gods started. Scared of the boogeyman, we needed a bigger, badder boogeyman to protect us."

He seemed to relish the conversation. "Religions are irrational love affairs with gods you can't see or prove with scientific methods. Sophisticated ghost stories; I like that. But I also see the need for the values that all the religions give us. Though we make the values up, they give meaning. I'm not sure if the world were only comprised of atheists it would survive. It would be like a gigantic Mad Max movie of chaos."

Abby may have seen that the whole conversation had me a little down, so he tried to bring some cheer back in. "Enough of the religious stuff. Who knows really? Why don't you give me another hour on the site? You might make another big discovery." He motioned toward the bank but down and away from the protruding skeleton. I followed him obediently, hoping to shake what had become a downer of a talk.

As I settled in the bank again, probing, brushing very delicately, I asked one of the students a ways up from me why they had picked this area to start with.

Suzanne was her name. She was a short, but full-bodied girl with sinewy arms. Pronounced veins ran like adventurous roots down them; the kind of definition weight lifters would die for. Her face was full, with especially pronounced, almost sensuous lips. A bandanna kept the sweat from her eyes.

"We really came to this location as archeologists to look at what Doctor Cole thinks is a 500 year old Indian religious center. The owners of the land were clearing out the area above the bank for hunting deer and found some pottery. Doctor Cole got a call because he is an expert on the early indigenous populations in Georgia."

"You mean he's both a paleontologist and an archeologist? I'm no scientist, but I thought these were very specialized fields."

"They are, but in Georgia there aren't many of either, and he is recognized as being quite reliable at both," she answered.

I questioned, "So you were up top looking for an Indian village and came down to the river and saw what?"

"First of all, Doctor Cole believes the Spanish explorer Hernando de Soto came through this part of Georgia in 1542, and wants to prove he did. That would create a stir in 1500's archeology. And, yes, we students came down for a swim at the end of work one day, and I saw what looked like a bone sticking out of the bank. That got us shifting from looking for something 500 years old to something millions of years old."

"So did you find anything up top?"

"Oh, we did. We had been up there for a month and found several very significant discoveries. We found Spanish beads that confirmed de Soto came here. But the really exciting find was a tiny cross they left or lost."

A jowly young man on the other side of me with undisguised disgust said, "Yeah, and then Suzanne lost it."

"Jerry, say that again, and I swear I'll slap you with this trowel," she shot back. Her cheery demeanor had changed in a flash.

"Well, you were the last one I saw carrying it to the photo table," he said accusingly.

"The cross was never in the box with the beads," she snapped, obviously upset that she was being accused of losing a critical piece of evidence that the Spanish had been here.

"Hey!" Abby yelled from down the way. "Cool it. We're a team here. Accidents happen. The beads prove what we came after."

I asked Suzanne, although with some reluctance, "I'm sure you all really searched for it."

"We went over the dig up there with a fine tooth comb, including the piles of dirt we had sifted through for a week. We took off half a day looking. I'm afraid it's gone. And it was a remarkable find." Her face fell in its sadness.

At noon Abby announced, "Okay. We've had a great morning. Let's break for lunch."

As the students grabbed their lunch sacks and headed for the shade of an enormous oak, I said to Abby, "You may not believe it, but I found the undeniable proof that God exists."

He smiled. "Good. I'm ready to be convinced. What's the proof?"

"Barbecue," I proclaimed. "Only a loving God could have created pulled pork and the sauce that goes on it. I passed a barbecue hole-in-the-wall a few miles back up the highway. I need to get out of the way, and my arteries need some grease."

He nodded emphatically, "Well, praise the Lord. That's the proof I've been seeking. Yeah, I thought I was in heaven at Fat Billy's back up the road."

We both let out those half laughs that are more breath than sound.

"Would you mind if I took a look at the Indian site up there before I go?" I asked.

He pointed to his left. "Sure. Take that path up the bank, but don't dare step on any part of the site. We'll be back up to work on it at mid afternoon."

I scurried up a pathway. The bank was a good twenty feet above the river, and at the top on flat ground I could see the site. *Dig* is the wrong descriptive noun for most of what happens when ancient ground is excavated. The scrub and grasses are stripped clean with only topsoil showing. Then the most meticulous scraping with small trowels starts on hands and knees with eyes peeled to the ground, looking for the slightest hint of an artifact.

A smallish, maybe 10 x 10 foot initial area is selected; strings break it into grids that can be numbered. Once the ground has been scrapped level, it presents ground as flat and clean and exquisitely smooth as a tabletop. Then delicate, narrow trenching down through the flat area starts. And this, like the flat area, is a methodical process of peeling back dirt no thicker than a potato peel. The purpose of this care is to discover artifacts without breaking them more than they might already be and to keep the dig going down at a level pace.

I could see broken pottery pieces barely sticking up here and there on the flat areas and in the six-inch deep, foot wide trenches. It can be a backbreaking enterprise into the past, which yields its secrets only to the hardy and the careful.

And then it happened. I turned to walk along the edge and back to the river. My tennis shoe caught on a pine root that had been left at the edge of the excavation, and I fell forward in a sprawling fall out into a corner of the site. It happened so suddenly that I could only get one arm and hand to slow my crash onto the ground. But it didn't prevent my forehead from hitting the edge of the north side of the dig. I felt the coolness of the dirt and its smoothness against my cheek and then a rush of pain from what felt like a pointed rock I had hit.

I lay spread eagle over their sacred ground, feeling like I had betrayed Abby's trust and desecrated their work. How stupid. How careless. My fall had flattened the ropes that formed the all-important grid. This is bad. Real bad, I thought.

Waiting for a moment to make sure I hadn't broken any bones, I raised my head and saw a small spot of blood on the ground.

Touching my forehead just inside the hairline, I felt broken skin and saw blood on my fingers when I drew them in front of me.

"What the devil," I uttered, and started slowly getting to my knees. I looked around for the rock, or maybe a piece of sharp-edged pottery and saw a sparkle on the edge of the trench where blood spotted. Angry at whatever the object was, I was determined to dig it out and throw it as far as I could.

I took my car keys out and started scrapping around the object. It first looked like a one inch little shiny stob sticking out of the compressed dirt, and then, "What is this," I muttered first. Then, "What is this!" I yelled. It was a small silver cross.

Abby responded in a distant voice, "What's the matter?"

I got up with the small silver cross in my hand and walked over to the edge of the bank. I looked down at him and the team who were all staring up, wondering what the yelling was about.

"Is this it?" I asked excitedly. "Look!" And I held it up for them to see.

That started them yelling and giving one another high fives. Abby yelled. "I don't believe it! Don't dare move. We're coming up."

They came scrambling up the bank then approached me almost cautiously, as though they didn't want to be disappointed. And then they saw it lying dirt-encrusted in my hands. Abby gingerly plucked it out and looked at me, shaking her head. "Where in the world did you find this?"

I turned and walked over to the spot. Everyone could see the carefully measured off ropes were in disarray, looking like spaghetti swirls in the dirt. "Listen, gang, I am so sorry I messed up your site. I don't know how to…"

"Are you kidding," Abby exclaimed. "This cross is undeniable verification that de Soto was here. Amazing!" he shouted.

"Dive in again. Maybe you'll uncover something else," Suzanne said, obviously relieved it had been found. They all laughed and started encouraging me to jump in. I had discovered a new way to explore a site—belly flop.

The group concluded someone had dropped the cross, no names mentioned, and stepped on it, mashing it underneath the dirt. It was on an outer edge section that was not going to be dug anymore.

They all patted me on the shoulder and back, thanking me profusely, and grinning broadly in the victory of the find.

I wiped the blood patch off my head with my hand; it wasn't much. Abby looked hard at the cut and pronounced I was ready to travel.

He walked me away from the site and toward the trail that led me back to my car. "I don't think I've ever had a day like this on an excavation. A team member would have found the pelvis on the whale, but we may never have found the cross again. I don't believe in fate, but I swear you were supposed to be here today," he said.

"There is some weird stuff going on. Crosses keep finding me."

He looked at me quizzically, "Huh?"

"Every time I think that there is no meaning to our lives, a sign jumps up and pulls me back. The cross I found is just one in a series. The signs seemed to be timed." I shook my head. "It's all very weird."

"I vacillated like that for a long time, but no more. I have found a real peace in my disbelief in a God. Knowledge is my belief; helping these kids is my service. I'm good with where I am." His smile was of complete peace and contentment.

"I envy you, Abby. I'll land on one side of this, and I think it will be soon. I'm forcing an answer."

He looked at me and said firmly, "A man's got to know where he stands on life's most important question. But few do. And I don't know how you force faith, even if that's where you want to go."

"Maybe I've attended God's funeral and it's too depressing to admit."

He nodded, we shook hands and I left.

It sat small, just down off the highway. Uneven, chipped-paint clapboards barely clung to their rusted nails. The screen door had a healthy population of flies all gawking through the screen and sniffing the heavy aroma of cooking and basting pork. Fat Billy filled one end of the tiny, four table eating area where the counter was. He didn't seem to have a cash register or credit card machine, but did have a long barreled pistol resting threateningly at the counter's end. This meant Billy only took cash, and the revealed gun dared anyone to try and take it.

"Yount some poke?" He drawled with a voice as slow as the smoke curling off the ribs on a side grill.

"A pulled pork sandwich with some burned skin, please. And I'll take some slaw and those baked beans. And two pieces of white bread. Yes, and sweet tea." Here in this oak-smokey, semi-lit, bare-ly standing clapboard joint was a church; sacred ground for those who worship at these shrines to succulent meat, long cooked. It is food that challenges the openness of your arteries, but promises that if it stops your heart, you will die with a smile on your face.

At least I could claim entrance to *this* heaven.

The Message

I was underneath the courthouse in Covington, 40 miles from Atlanta. The timbers undergirding the courthouse were 12 x 12 inch yellow heart pine, a golden amber wood once used extensively as the steel for buildings in the 1800's. My cell vibrated from my shirt pocket. It was Callie.

"You'd better come on back. Jack took a real turn last night. He's back at Piedmont. They're saying he may have 24 hours."

"Is he conscious?"

"In and out. He'll suddenly be as aware and talking as we are, then out again. The family said he has asked for you several times. He calls you his messenger. So, what is it?"

If I had been with her, I would have seen the confusion on her pretty face as I heard it in her voice. "Is it a good message?" Her voice lifted in anticipation.

"Let's talk about it tomorrow," I avoided her.

"Okay, but I'll bet it's good news." She desperately wanted me to join the team.

Her voice then modulated to one more serious. "I've already been in the waiting room an hour, commiserating with friends. The waiting room is packed. Betty came out and visited. There will be a number of us in a prayer group in the hospital's chapel if you don't see me when you come."

Praying for what, I wanted to say. He's dying. He's dead. Is the prayer for some miraculous turnaround? Are you asking for divine intervention? Is God sitting and waiting for the heartbroken

to beg him to alter events? Then does that mean he is capricious
and can have his mind changed? Miracles for the asking, I sarcastically thought. And can we pray a man uncertain of God into God's
forgiveness? Is being a proxy, a stand in for the sinner, okay? But I
avoided that crossing of swords and said, "I'll be there in an hour."

My ship was bearing me to a reckoning. When I reached the
hospital, I had to be prepared to confront my devils of doubt and
the angels that begged conviction to the faith. No more squish.
No more maybe, maybe not. Jack was on the final glide path, and
he expected my explorations to have unearthed a singular landing
place. And that place was the word *yes*. Yes, Jack, there is a loving God who pared off a part of himself, called him My Son and
sent him in human form to offer forgiveness and eternal life. Yes,
there is a bona fide meaning to life. We aren't just soup in a skin
container.

I knew as I drove exactly what Jack wanted, what he needed in his final, terrified breaths to hear. But on what shore had I
landed? And how pathetic it is to still be asking this question after
a summer's pilgrimage? But I bore the burden; a responsibility that
began as a winsome inquiry into how we all might retire, then,
unexpectedly, into an odyssey to find if we ultimately survive or
dissipate into nothingness.

And where was I, the good messenger? What was my message to be? I thought I would take the time to sort through the last
two months while I drove. I had definitely found Jesus the man in
all of his complexities. If he were to be for every man, perhaps he
had to be every man. Except he had no meanness or duplicity as
we do.

He was a man of contradictions as are we. A rebel but a con-
formist. A brilliant analyzer of the needs, greed and worries of
the people of his era, yet one impatient with their reluctance to

change. A leader who could take the old and present it as new as he did with the Old Testament and the prophets. A communicator who knew the power of the meal as a relationship-builder and as a lubricant for teaching and convincing. Sensitive and compassionate as a woman or as one wounded deeply as a child. Flamboyant and shy. Insistent yet forgiving. A showman and a loner. But fierce. Was he ever fierce in his drive to deliver his message.

Armed with no armor, I would open myself to Max and Phil. I would share what my pretend older Jesus had to say for them. I had found on this journey that at times of difficulty someone else can form our words, the demons within us or the gods or The God. We are vessels, messengers for another's message. And I could feel a long-away Message moving toward me.

I dialed Max while I drove toward Atlanta. "You on the way?" he asked tersely.

"Yeah, sounds like you're in the waiting room. Step away from them. I've got something to tell you." I could hear voices around him.

Then the voices diminished. "There's quite a crowd here. I've led several prayers for his soul. We gotta help our buddy whether he believes or not. We've all been in to his room one and two at a time to say goodbye. Man, this is the toughest thing I've ever been through. He's leaving the foursome," his voice cracked.

"Max, I have a message for you from my research over the summer."

"Sonny, Jack is dying. Let's worry about me another time." Max said impatiently.

"No, it has to be now," I insisted. "It's based on your commitment to Christ, a man who appeared to have changed his life's course in his mid thirties. He stopped working. He built a ministry on nothing but the good will of those he touched. You do the same.

Give up the things that are burdening you. Get rid of the unsold houses. Let the banks take them back. Start all over. Start a ministry among construction workers and builders. This recession has destroyed their lives just as it is taking the joy out of your life. Start a construction business discipleship."

There was a pause that went so long I thought I had lost his signal. Then he said in a lugubrious tone, "Our boy is dying and you're telling me to go bankrupt and become a preacher. Are we on the same planet?"

I relented. "You know the pain, Max. Jesus taught from pain. Use yours like he did to bring relief to others. Quit the club. You can't afford the fees anymore anyway. Live with less, but give more from your experiences. Take this beating and show the scars it has given you to others in your business, then tell how your belief has eased the pain."

Another long pause, then in a hushed rebuttal, "It's not that simple, Sonny. There's the wife, the private schools, the club; they keep me sane. They're my sanctuaries. I need cash, friend, big time. I've already got Christ."

This wasn't the time to debate what Max should do with the rest of his life. I had said what my journey had told me I should say to Max. I had become too convinced of his commitment. I had listened too often to his pronouncements of Christ's love. I forgot how human Max is and how realties are often what we make them. Max was very good, I now realized, at compartmentalizing his life. Christ in this drawer. His business in another. His golf here, family there.

"I'll be there in a few minutes. We can get into this later," I said.

"You're not coming here to talk to me. You're Jack's designated messenger. He's slipping fast. The news has gotta be good.

There better be a lot of Jesus in this message, a lot of asking for for-giveness and for grace. He needs a deathbed confession big time."

We hung up. I hated this whole situation. Am I supposed to float like an apparition, an angel, into his room and smile beatifi-cally, raise my hands like Jesus does in his pictures or the Pope does when he blesses people and say, 'Repent and you're saved, my son'.

I then called Phil. He was on the practice range. "What the hell are you doing hitting golf balls? Why aren't you at the hospi-tal?" I asked in disbelief.

"Been there, done that," he answered laconically.

"So did you see Jack?" I asked.

"Yes. He looked small and white." Phil was speaking tersely, as though he wanted to avoid the subject.

"Did ya'll talk?" I was trying to communicate.

"I went to his room. His daughter said 'Phil's here, Jack.' He opened his eyes and whispered, 'Go hit balls.'"

"That was it? No mourning, no handholding, no pats on the head, no heartfelt words? Go hit balls?" I was incredulous.

Phil answered, "That's all he said, or muttered. I said, 'It's all fairways and greens for you, Jack,' then turned around and left and came here to the practice range, where I'm honoring my friend's deathbed request."

To me, a touching command from Jack to get the hell out of that depressing room, away from the fleeing of a life, and go do something that defied the coming death. Phil was not one to show much emotion, but I suspect it was a grim practice he was having.

"Phil, I want to give you a message," I said, though I felt an-other's voice was saying the words.

"What message? From whom?"

"From me. From my search this summer. You know the Je-sus as an old man thing."

"Oh, boy. Here we go. Sonny's going Jesus on me. Words from the road to save the sinner who doesn't believe in sin. Save the preaching for Jack, Sonny."

"No, hear me out. I found there is good news for you nihilists, and you already know it," I insisted.

"Hey, the man knows a new word. Sounds like the search for Jesus became an educational tour."

"It did. Got me to thinking deeper than the inch I've been thinking at," I admitted.

"I'm proud of you, buddy. I'm always amused that I know more about a religion than the people that believe in it know." Phil believed Christians to be skimmers.

Before I could respond, it sounded like the phone suddenly hit the ground. There was a pause then the unmistakable sweet sound of driver on ball; then the rustling of his picking up his cell phone out of the grass.

"That beauty was for the Jackster," Phil bragged after obviously hitting a great fairway shot.

"Okay, here's my message for you, Phil. You don't believe life has meaning or purpose; that we create values and morality to give life meaning. And you believe until a man comes to grips with that reality that his life will be chaotic and unhappy."

"You must have checked my man Nietzsche out." Phil gave one of his typical half joke responses.

"I did," I said. "I have thought a lot about what if this life is pointless. No God. All physics and chemistry. It's the kind of thought that keeps people up at night, and it has scared the stuff out of Jack. But it's one you are comfortable with, so use that peace you have come to."

You can tell when someone is walking while talking on a cell phone. I could hear the breeze outside Phil's voice. He said, "It's been a mental roller coaster for me, I'll admit. I was raised in the Methodist church. I followed the path of my parents with no thought of whether I accepted that path or not. In college I found a greater wonder in how our universe works, not why it works, or who might be behind its creation. I just was awe-struck at the evolving creation."

"And that didn't translate into believing God created it and was guiding it?" I asked. We can know people intimately and yet never know them. Men are surface riders, yuk-it-uppers, back slappers. We dwell on flimsy queries: how's business, is the market going to crash again, what's your handicap, did you see that woman?

"No, the more I learned the less God made sense. It was kind of my Santa Claus moment. It was depressing, unnerving. I felt an utter emptiness and vulnerability. I went through a very dark period, and then emerged in a form of worship." Phil has never revealed himself like this.

"Worship? Worship of what?" I asked.

"The exquisite complexity and beauty of life. I realized the way out of my depression about a pointless world was to become a lifelong student, a worshipper if you will, of life's intricate and interwoven nature. I have found great joy in being what I call myself, a wonder wanderer."

"And that's my message. You are not a follower of Jesus, but you can follow his example. Spread hope to those who see no meaning in a meaningless world. Start an association or club that honors, that worships the workings of nature. Honor your belief, for you do have a belief, in the quality of life."

The phone fell into the grass again. The sweet sound of metal on ball and the muffled retrieval of the phone. "Another high arching fade pin high for Jack. What'd you say? Spread some cheer to the cheerless? Jesus in camouflage? I like that, my boy."

He paused and asked rhetorically, "Can you live a happy life believing there is no purpose to any of this?"

How ironical that life's ultimate question is the one question that is almost never asked.

"No, I can't," I answered. "I'm a complete coward about that. I gotta have something to lean on."

"Then you had better find you a religion. And if it's Christianity, I wouldn't pursue it just because you're afraid of no hereafter. That would be selfish and the many readings of the gospels I've done say life's meaning is not about you so much as it is Christ and your love for Him."

I had become amazed at how thorough this atheist knew what my faith was supposed to be about.

Could I surrender before I got to the hospital? Or could I acknowledge I could never believe the Bible's story and create my own meaning for life; a code that said be good. Be caring and compassionate and giving. And forget the ending. Live within each moment, finding joy in the creation. Or had I in fact found Him, and am now working out the kinks, so to speak?

We live close to the hospital, so I stopped by our house for a final act of immaturity. I would fix my dying buddy and myself a going-away drink. In my Starbuck's thermos I made a Bloody Mary. I always kept a fifth of vodka in the freezer, so this drink would remain cold. I would offer a dying man his last drink. It was our way, as childish and irreverent as it might seem.

Piedmont Hospital has become a sprawling series of unadorned red brick buildings, a campus where death and pain are joined in minute by minute combat by skilled hands and miraculous medicines. An icon in Buckhead, Piedmont, as it is called, is a testimony to life and new births that ironically sits on what was once a killing field during the Battle of Atlanta in the Civil War.

My mind had been noticeably calm as I drove in from Covington. I almost felt removed from Jack's passing. I felt immune from death and illness, invulnerable to the destruction of cells and body parts. Why can the failure of others make us feel strong? But as I saw the hospital campus sitting low at the top of a hill on Peachtree Road, I felt buried under a tumulus of grief. I felt a dread so suffocating I sat in the car breathing deeply, flushed with the pain of loss. Would he die while I watched? What would it be like? I shook my head at the selfishness of the moment. I had words to say, a responsibility to meet.

The halls are wide; the tile floors so clean they are almost mirrors. I stepped off the fourth floor elevator and into the waiting room. There were a large number of our friends sitting and standing, speaking, whispering, saying nothing, all in quiet deference to the passage-taking place down the hall.

I hugged several of them, shook hands with others, some I didn't know. What do you say? Words don't work here. Watchmen watch in silence for the coming enemy. I soon slipped away to see him, although I was told it was now family only. The enemy was close at hand.

I walked with no eagerness. What would I say? What had I discovered? Would I simply lie?

The door to his room was signed with "Family Only." I tapped and his twenty-something son Bryan opened it slightly.

"Oh, Sonny, glad you're here," he welcomed me with sincerity. "Dad's asked for you. He keeps saying you're the good messenger. What's that all about?"

I wanted to ignore the question so I started to say something, then acted like his mother had summoned me, and I moved away.

Hospital rooms are spare. Just containers for bodies in various stages of birth or battle. Flowers garnered the room in quiet celebration. Jack's mother sat by the wide window, a hazy white thing of nicely coiffed hair, but brittle looking and slightly bent. She offered a fixed, beatific smile at me; a reluctant angel delegated to assist in the travel into the next land. Hold the hand. Say 'You can go now'. It is finished.

The other sentinel at the gate was his wife Betty. She stood next to the bed as though she would be called upon by some requester to do something; suddenly comfort him, take his hand, wet a cloth, plump the covers. What do those on The Watch do? Stand, sit, walk in small shuffles around the small room. Stare at the loved one. Pray for God's great hand to intervene. Listen for noises, words. We are gauges measuring all movements and utterances. And as we make the calls of the passing to friends and family, we will be asked to give those measurements of time and space, of last moves and words and sounds and appearances.

It was mid afternoon. The sun was swooning behind the building, but the August light found full acceptance in the room. Jack was cocooned under a tightly wrapped sheet and light blanket. It made his six-foot frame appear more compact and narrow than it was. His head, hair carefully combed, was slightly elevated on the plumpness of a pillow.

Betty reached out to me with her right hand, saying nothing, but with a smile lit with tears. Her hand took mine and pulled me over to the bed. A lonely word or two were ushered between us, a perfunctory salutation, "Thank you for coming." Well-meaning meaninglessness.

She touched Jack's shoulder and spoke with some energy, even anticipation. Was there a hope for rescue in her voice? "Jack, guess who's here? It's Sonny. Or should I say the good messenger?" She looked at me with an obvious 'What's this all about' expression.

Jack's eyes fluttered like the wings of a lazy dove in half-hearted flight. He looked up at me, and a Jack-of-old smile creased across his face. He looked at his mother, waved his fingers up like he was swooshing something away and ordered without the usual energy of an order, "Outside. Got to tell war stories; don't want the faint of heart to hear." It was the original Jack, cutting up, kidding, a bon vivant.

But it was pretense. The family left in slow motion, heavily cloaked in grief. Jack's face turned fierce as they closed the door behind them.

His hand, punctured by fixed needles, gripped my wrist and asked with such determination as I felt I was now imprisoned in the room by his unquenchable desire to know. His voice was weak and in a monotone, but still had an edge when he simply asked, "And?"

Implicit within that one word was the question of the ages: is there a meaning to this life and if so, what is it? What an absurdity for me to have been asked that question, and an even greater absurdity that after an intensive search, my mind remained a redundancy of doubt. The words would have to be their own living things, forming and carrying themselves out as they alone determined, and informing me as well as Jack.

Again he whispered, "Put the pressure on you, didn't I? Go find if God exists. Not like, bring me back a coffee, easy on the cream."

I felt a quick anger, and my voice betrayed it. "You did put pressure on me and I didn't want it. I have no qualifications to be telling you whether you should start praying your butt off because there is a heaven, or forget it, because there isn't."

His responses were delayed, because he had to summon his energies to say anything. "You cussing out a dying man?" He tried a small laugh, but it sounded more like a rasping cough.

"And?" he persistently whispered the word in a long breath.

He was trying to wrench honesty out of me on a subject I've been a life-long liar about. I didn't want the responsibility of telling this dying man, or any man, if he should pray in some last minute desperation that there was a loving God to bestow forgiveness on his lifelong doubt.

And then I started thinking that this had been a journey guided by a series of signs. Each had moved me further away from my original search for an older Jesus toward something more troubling; just what do I believe about anything? And to paraphrase Jesus, *just who do I think I am?*

"Jack, I've been moved by signs, or as we would have called it, some very weird things have happened. I'm reminded of a statement by Jesus on how we need to have eyes to see. You could argue that much of life is what you are open to seeing. You and I have thought that these signs and miracles are just more of the Christian buffet of baloney."

"What signs?" he asked. I had to read his lips for his mumbling to make any sense.

"Actually, I'm finding signs everywhere, starting with us finding that cross back in June. I've even cut my head on a cross. And then there's this very strange man that everybody thinks is dead."

I pulled the thermos jug off the table, unscrewed the top and realized how stupid it was to offer him a drink, so I took a slug myself, as he winked at my eternal frat boy actions.

I held the thermos up, and said, "Here's to you, dear friend. Here's to happy endings."

His eyes fluttered. I thought he was falling asleep, but he rallied enough to ask with a persistence that a dying body could not stop, "So?"

His one word question had reduced life to its essence. Single words can do that; contain encyclopedias of information. Love. Hate. Yes. No. And? So? Premeditation didn't form my answer. The words came of their own independent creation and energy.

"Jack, my head has always said *no*. But the heart, my heart, says *yes*, even though a lot of this is still a mystery to me."

"Yes," crept across his mouth, pushing it into a near grin. "Keep yes, Sonny. Hold on to it now that you've found it."

For no reason to me my eyes suddenly watered up. I felt it and my vision blurred through the tearing, and Jack saw it and for whatever it meant to him, he nodded ever so slightly. I put my hand over his fingers and we stared at one another for a long, quiet moment.

Jack then turned his head toward the window. His breathing became quicker and without depth, and he stayed turned toward the window.

What had happened here? I never really answered, or did I? *'Yes'* can be an answer so shallow and undefined, but maybe for this moment, it made a powerful and comprehensive statement. Should I have lied and said I now have the unalterable conviction that this universe is not some cosmic joke, and that a loving God is real? But would it have been a lie if I had said that?

I was at once deeply disappointed in myself, but then again, I wasn't. Maybe my plight is to forever question. That's my nature— to question, be skeptical, not cynical, but forever exploring and digging for the truth on a subject or a person. I can find conviction on many subjects, but on this most important one, I may forever be a wanderer, one day awash and lost, the next standing on firm ground. But I'll push for that position that life does have meaning and it's through the God of my childhood.

A tap on the door and Betty peeped through it's opening. "Okay, golfers, enough of the locker room talk," she said with a chirpy façade.

I stood and faced her and put my finger to my lips to indicate he might be asleep. Softly I said, "It was a great visit. It meant a lot to me. You're kind to have given us the time." Looking back at his peaceful form, I said, "I think I bored him to sleep."

I kissed her on the cheek, gave her son a hug, nodded to several other family members entering and left.

I knew I would never see Jack alive again.

Did I fail as a messenger? And what were those tears all about? Was the message in my tears? Or in the unexplained word *yes*. Is this all of the conclusion I could give him? If so, it wasn't consciously delivered by me. But he saw the tears, and his face changed. Was that the moment when he accepted God's grace, or did he feel they were tears of disappointment that I had found nothing, though I did say *'Yes?'* I left the room feeling a strange peace, a peace that I had finished this particular journey. I had found the shore I was hoping for, whether I was ready to admit it or not.

I have never had such a pleasant ride home, but I suspect it wasn't half as pleasant as Jack's.

CPSIA information can be obtained at www.ICGtesting.com
Printed in the USA
LVOW041410300512

283936LV00001B/6/P